How to get onto the property

A first-time buyer's guide to financing and finding your first home

ISBN: 9781702354257

Ned Browne

How to get onto the property ladder
© Ned Browne 2019

About the author

Ned Browne spent his early career working for some of London's best-known advertising agencies including Saatchi & Saatchi, TBWA and Collett Dickenson Pearce, helping create award-winning campaigns and developing strengths in marketing, branding and digital. Latterly, he has worked in journalism, property development/consultancy, brand and product development, online marketing and education.

Ned Browne is also the Reader's Digest's long-term property correspondent. He has advised numerous would-be property owners, helping many get onto the property ladder.

By the same author:

Love University - How to survive and thrive at university

The A-Z of Amazon.co.uk FBA - *A step-by-step guide to branding, sourcing and selling private-label FBA products on Amazon's UK website*

Part 1 - Financing your first property purchase

Part 5 - Moving into your first property

Appendix

Introduction

Things have never been tougher for first-time buyers. The number of people aged 25-34 who own their own home has more than halved since 1996. But aspirations are still high. Santander's First-Time Buyer Study collected data from over 5,000 non-homeowning adults aged 18-40 years. Over 90% aspired to owning their own home and it was the "top life goal" for 51% of those surveyed. Unfortunately, 70% of would-be first-time buyers believe the dream of homeownership is already over for many young people. This has given rise to "generation rent" - those people who believe they will be renting for their entire lives. For some people that's a lifestyle choice; for others it has been forced upon them by rising property prices. Still more people feel trapped by the ever-increasing cost of renting and the long waiting lists for the dwindling number of council properties. In addition, recent market uncertainty has put off other first-time buyers, who are concerned that property prices may fall in the future.

Owning a place you can call home is hugely emotive. In 1914, just 10% of people owned their own homes. This rose to a touch over 70% in 2003, until falling back to 63% in recent years. We are still a nation of homeowners, but now it's the first-time buyers who are struggling.

I have written this book to help young people get onto the property ladder. For most, this will not be easy. But knowledge is power. Read on.

Part 1 - Financing your first property purchase

Does buying make financial sense?

This is not an easy question to answer. Even in boom years there are winners and losers. But you can protect yourself from possible downsides. And, in the long run, being a homeowner will almost certainly make you better off. MORE TH>N, an insurance company, used to publish an annual Cost of Running a Home report. The interesting point was that the annual cost of ownership and renting were always remarkably similar. But the report did not look at different life stages. Those retiring as mortgage-free homeowners do not pay a mortgage, nor do they pay rent. Conversely, those renting into retirement face the dual problem of a fixed pension alongside rising rents. As life expectancy has risen, so has the number of pensioners living in poverty. Moreover, retired homeowners have an asset, often their most valuable asset.

But, for most, the financial upside of long-term homeownership should be even more significant. If average prices rose just 2.5% a year (which is way below historic trends), the average property would double in value in 28 years. During this time, most people would have hoped to have paid off their mortgages.

This is not to say buying a property guarantees a prosperous future. There are countless tales of properties being repossessed, people being stuck in homes they cannot sell, and of homeowners enduring years of negative equity. This book aims to help you avoid making mistakes that can cost you dear.

Buying your first property is no easy task, unless you are fortunate enough to have wealthy parents. Even then, who wants to lose money? But it can be broken down into numerous small tasks, which should be far more manageable.

Property vs. the stock market
Some people advocate putting your money into the stock market over property. Indeed, journalists often cite figures that show the stock market has produced better returns over certain periods in history. But this is lazy journalism, as these figures assume the same amount of money will be available to invest in both. Consider this: no business is going to lend you £250,000 to invest in the stock market. But you may be able to borrow the same amount to purchase a property.

Here's a worked example:
Given that you can't borrow £250,000 to invest in the stock market, you will need to invest money each month instead. If you invested £6,000 a year (i.e. £500 a month) and the stock market grew, on average, by 5% a year, after 20 years you would make approximately £95,000 profit.

However, you may be able to borrow £250,000 to buy a property. If you did so, and property prices went up by just 2.5% a year (half the stock market example above), after 20 years the property would have risen in value by approximately £160,000. If property prices rose by 5% a year during that period, your property would have risen in value by a whopping £413,000.
Plus you could use the £500 a month you haven't paid into the stock market to pay off your mortgage. Over 20 years that would total £120,000.
Yes, you have to make interest payments on your mortgage borrowing. But you also have to pay rent if you don't buy.

I am not saying you should not invest in the stock market - you should; it's good to have a diverse portfolio of investments. But, from a standing start, it's hard to make significant gains, especially in the short term.

Other reasons to buy

Security. Those renting are, to a certain extent, at the mercy of their landlord or landlady. Recent changes to laws have given tenants more security and greater access to longer tenancies. However, many renters find themselves having to move every few years. Plus, tenants are subject to rent rises.

Have it how you want it. If you own your own property, you can paint the walls pink (if you so desire). You can also put pictures up, change the furniture and hold parties without the risk of eviction.

Rent is dead money. If you rent an average two bedroom flat in London, you will pay over £800,000 in rent over 30 years. Over the same period, if you rented in Burnley (the cheapest place to rent in the UK) you can expect to pay over £200,000.

An Englishman's home is his castle. The same applies to women, the Welsh, the Scottish and the Irish. Coming home to a property *you own* makes those long days at work all seem worthwhile.

Cheap money. The interest charged on mortgages is low, as the property is used as collateral for the mortgage debt. Having access to inexpensive money should save you tens of thousands of pounds of interest during the course of your lifetime.

Some downsides of buying a property

Lack of flexibility. Renting allows you to do the following more easily: move jobs, take career breaks or work abroad. Homeowners need to think more carefully about such moves. But, provided there is a healthy rental market in your area, you can always let out your property (with permission from your lender) if a big life change is looming.

Repossession. If you do not keep up with your monthly mortgage payments, your property risks being repossessed. Homeownership is definitely more suited to those who are disciplined with their money.

Negative equity. If property prices fall, you may find yourself with an asset that's worth less than the outstanding mortgage.

Added responsibility. You will be responsible for managing and repairing the property. Learning some DIY skills is a must.

Should I wait for property prices to fall?

No one can predict what will happen to property prices. Some people will wait for prices to fall only to see them rise out of their reach. Others will be more lucky. But, remember, property ownership is not just a long-term investment; it's far more than that. Over your lifetime, property prices will peak and trough. Provided you are able to pay the mortgage every month, you can ride out any storm.

Moreover, a significant fall in property prices could actually negatively affect first-time buyers. Banks would reign in their lending and would most likely require you to save a larger deposit. Also, it would almost certainly lead to a loss in consumer confidence and an economic downturn - leading to higher unemployment and lower wage growth. On the flipside, further astronomical property price rises could further fuel the rise in social and generational divide. Here's hoping we see very modest price rises from now on. That way, everyone wins.

How much can I borrow?

In the world of property, borrowing money is a necessary evil. The important thing to remember is that money makes money. Obviously you hope that, as time goes by, you will start to pay back this debt and your salary will rise (as will the value of the property). Thus your mortgage payments will become more manageable.

So, how much can you borrow? This used to be simple: a single person could borrow 3½ times their salary and a couple could borrow 2½ times their combined salaries. But a lot of reckless lending took place in the run-up to the 2008 credit crunch. In the United Kingdom we had self-certification mortgages, which effectively enabled borrowers to invent their salary (they were banned in 2011). In the USA they had what became known as NINJA loans (a play on No Income No Assets). Before the 2008 financial crisis, lending rules were fairly relaxed in many countries across the world. It was reckless lending that caused the sub-prime mortgage fiasco in the USA. If you'd like to understand this better, I urge you to watch the film The Big Short (or read the book). This sub-prime lending gave rise to the global financial crisis, and resulted in a raft of more stringent lending rules. The end result is this: it's now much harder to get a mortgage. From 2014 all lenders have been required to conduct full affordability checks on mortgage applicants. This could involve an in-depth look at day-to-day outgoings, including student loans and credit card debt. Some over-enthusiastic lenders have questioned applicants about haircut costs, gambling habits, pocket-money commitments and even charity donations. Lenders also "stress test" the loan – could the applicant afford to pay if interest rates rose?

So there is no fixed answer to the question: how much can I borrow? But there is a rough range. Banks and building societies will usually lend between 3½ and 4½ times total annual household income. So, if you're single and earn £50,000 you could expect to be able to borrow between £175,000 and £225,000. A couple with a combined income of £75,000 could expect to be able to borrow between £262,500 and £337,500.

What if I'm self-employed?
It's much tougher to get a mortgage if you do not have a full-time job. Mortgage lenders like certainty and believe guaranteed long-term income is the best way to ensure this. So, if you're self-employed, a contract worker or you've worked abroad, expect to jump through more hoops.

Lenders are also wary of people on short-term contracts or those on a probation period at work. To be frank, if you have recently started working for yourself, obtaining a mortgage will be pretty much impossible. However, if you have a track record of self employment, you will need to prove your earnings. Typically, you will need to provide the following paperwork:

- **Your business accounts**. Most lenders will require three years of signed-off accounts. The lender will be assessing your profits, not your turnover. Of course, as a business owner it's often best to try to minimise your profits by, for example, reinvesting in the business, to minimise your tax bill. However, while this is good business sense, it will not help you get a mortgage. This is far from ideal.

- **Your tax returns**. If you do not have business accounts, some lenders will accept your tax returns. Again, most lenders will want three years' worth.
- **Other ad-hoc evidence**. If you're self-employed you may be asked to provide a range of additional evidence. Some lenders will be more demanding than others. If you are in this position, I urge you to use a mortgage advisor (more on mortgage advisors later) as they will know the lenders that are most likely to approve your application.

Note: If you have a partner who is not self-employed, this may increase your chances of obtaining a mortgage.

Clubbing together
It's possible for up to four people to own a property jointly. If you find yourself completely priced out of your desired location, this might be an option. Oddly enough, once you have one mortgage it is far easier to get another one. So, getting a buy-to-let mortgage on an investment property is far more likely if you have a residential mortgage. As such, buying with family members and friends is definitely something to consider.

Loan to Value (LTV)
Many mortgages have a maximum Loan To Value. In simple terms this refers to the maximum, as a percentage of the property's value, the lender is willing to lend.
So, for example, if the maximum Loan To Value was 90% and the property was priced at £300,000, the mortgage lender would loan a maximum of £270,000 (i.e. 90% of £300,000). The best mortgage rates are invariably offered to

people with the lowest Loan To Value percentage. As a first-time buyer, this is pretty grating.

The deposit
The deposit is the lump sum of cash you invest into the property purchase. Because of Loan to Value requirements, almost all mortgages require the borrower to have a deposit. Buyers with larger deposits will have more borrowing options. This means they will be able to access the best (i.e. lowest) interest rates. This is because banks like you to have skin in the game - if they are risking their money, they want you to risk your money too. Moreover, a larger deposit should help prevent you from falling into negative equity.
At a minimum you should try to save a 5% deposit. Banks are keen to attract first-time buyers, and putting down this much money shows you are financially prudent. Saving for a deposit is no mean feat. In fact, for many people it is the biggest hurdle to property ownership they face. You have to make sacrifices, sometimes for years - that means fewer holidays, less going out, fewer new clothes, etc. Indeed, you should question everything you buy. The important thing is this: start now and save every time you get paid.

Top tip: Put down just slightly more than the minimum deposit amount. If you do so, your mortgage is more likely to be approved. So, if the minimum deposit stipulated was £30,000, put down £30,100.

Lifetime (Individual Savings Account) ISA
If you are saving for a deposit, you should put your savings into a Lifetime ISA, which can be used to buy your first home. Here's how it works:

- You must be 18 or over (but under 40) to open a Lifetime ISA.
- You can put in up to £4,000 each year, until you're 50. The Government will add a 25% bonus to your savings, up to a maximum of £1,000 per year.
- The Lifetime ISA limit of £4,000 counts towards your annual ISA limit (which currently stands at £20,000 per tax year).
- You can hold cash or stocks and shares in your Lifetime ISA, or have a combination of both.
- To open and continue to pay into a Lifetime ISA you must be a resident in the UK, unless you're a crown servant (for example, in the diplomatic service), their spouse or civil partner.
- You can withdraw money from your ISA if you're:
  - Buying your first home.
  - Aged 60 or over.
  - Terminally ill, with less than 12 months to live.
- You'll pay a 25% charge if you withdraw cash or assets for any other reason.
- You can use your savings to help you buy your first home if all the following apply:
  - The property costs £450,000 or less.
  - You buy the property at least 12 months after you open the Lifetime ISA.
  - You use a conveyancer or solicitor to act for you in the purchase.
  - You're buying with a mortgage.

The bank of mum and dad
You could also consider asking for help. If you have parents who are in a position to lend a hand, there is no harm in

asking. You would not be alone: more than 25% of all property purchases are funded or part funded by that most unorthodox of banks. But, be careful.

When Shakespeare penned the line "neither a borrower nor a lender be" he definitely had a point. Money is one of the biggest causes of family disputes. As a rule, you need to consider whether your parents could afford to lose this money. If the answer is no, this is not the right path. If the answer is yes, this may well be prudent financial planning. Currently, if a person's estate is worth over £325,000 they are liable for inheritance tax on everything over that amount – at a rate of 40%. That threshold has not risen for some time, despite rapidly rising property prices. As a result, many more people now have estates worth more than the inheritance tax threshold. This is something to consider.

The average "loan" to children is almost £25,000. As such, you need to be aware of the inheritance tax implications. If the money is genuinely a loan, it's important appropriate documentation is put in place that will satisfy the taxman – this will also help avoid possible future family disputes.

If it's a gift, there are other implications: everyone has an annual inheritance tax gift allowance that enables parents to give money away without worrying about inheritance tax. The annual allowance is £3,000 per person. However, this is the benefactor's personal allowance – so, if you have siblings, they may want a slice of the action too. There's also a one-year carry over allowance – so if they haven't used their allowance one year, they can gift £6,000 the following year. If your parents decide to gift you more than the tax-free allowance, things get more complicated. If they die within seven years of making that gift, some inheritance tax will be payable under the "seven-year rule", which measures the number of years between the gift and their demise. This is how the "taper relief" is calculated:

Years between gift and inheritance tax paid

less than 3	40%
3 to 4	32%
4 to 5	24%
5 to 6	16%
6 to 7	8%
7 or more	0%

It would seem that the key advantage of borrowing money to get onto the property ladder is that it allows you to create wealth, as opposed to paying rent to a landlord. In other words, you're keeping money in the family. But tread carefully – anything with the potential to tear a family apart needs to be handled with kid gloves.

Interest rates
The most important factor when choosing a mortgage is the interest rate. The lower the interest rate, the less you will pay in interest each month. Each lender will decide its own rate of interest but, broadly speaking, all are influenced by the Bank of England's base rate.
Each month, the Bank of England's Monetary Policy Committee analyses a number of economic indicators such as economic growth, the rate of inflation and the level of unemployment and, based on these, decides the base rate.
If it thinks the economy is overheating it will increase interest rates and vice versa. This is, of course, a simplification, but it's what you need to know as a borrower, as any rises will directly impact you.

It's worth noting that, when the Bank of England lowered the base rate to a historic low of 0.5% on Thursday 5th March 2009, few would have predicted that they would still be below 1% a decade later. Bear in mind that interest rates have never before been below 1% since the Bank of England was founded in 1694.

So, while interest rates have remained low for a long time, there is no guarantee they will continue to do so. If you are concerned about the impact of future rate rises you should get your mortgage fixed for a long as possible, taking into account possible future changes in your personal circumstances. The mortgages available change on a daily basis and all borrowers should shop around for the best deal. Loyalty does not pay when it comes to mortgages. In fact, it rarely pays with any financial products.

Even if you have a repayment mortgage, you should also consider making additional over-payments every month. Almost all mortgages allow this, and you should not underestimate the value of compound interest. Here's a hypothetical example: if you overpaid £1,000 a month on a mortgage that charged 4% interest you would pay £144,000 less in interest payments over a 25-year period. It's a hypothetical example, as interest rates will vary during the course of 25 years, as will your ability to over pay - several other factors may vary too. But, you get the picture: overpaying will save you money in the long run.

Lessons from history

Many of you will have heard of the interest-rate hell of the early 1990s. The Government was struggling to control inflation and it's reckoned that two million people fell into negative equity. In 1991 an estimated 75,000 properties were repossessed – interest rates increased from 8% to 13%

in six months. Could this happen again? In the near term (let's say the next 20 years) this is highly unlikely. But, stranger things have happened.

There are two schools of thought when interest rates are low. The first is to borrow as much money as possible, invest in assets (such as property) and hope asset prices rise and interest rates stay low. The second is to use the opportunity to repay the loan capital as fast as possible (as you'll be spending less on the interest payments). Both approaches have merit - it really depends on your attitude to risk.

Low interest rates are the bane of all savers. But, in the property world, they are always welcomed with open arms.

What is a mortgage?

A mortgage is a form of long-term borrowing secured against a property. Some things to know about mortgages:

- As the loan is secured against the property, the rate of interest paid on mortgages is usually much lower than other forms of borrowing.
- However, if you fail to keep up with the mortgage payments, your lender can take possession of your property. This is known as being repossessed.
- Mortgages are a long-term form of borrowing. Most are paid back over a 25-year period.

Features of mortgages

There are lots of different types of mortgages. Here are the main things to consider:

- The rate of interest. This will determine your monthly mortgage payments, so getting the lowest rate of interest should be your main goal.
- Is the rate of interest fixed? If so, for how long?

- Mortgage fees. (More on mortgage fees later.)

The two most common types of mortgage are repayment and interest-only. Almost all first-time buyers will use one of these, so they will be my focus. But I will also cover other types of mortgage such as tracker, capped, offset and 100%.

Repayment mortgage
This is, as the name suggests, when your monthly payments cover the interest and a small part of the capital. Standard repayment mortgage terms are 25 years. This means that the monthly payment is calculated so that, after 25 years, you have paid off your mortgage. For most first-time buyers, a repayment mortgage is probably the best option.

Interest-only mortgage
This is a very simple mortgage product. You borrow the money and pay interest on that borrowing on a monthly basis. Your mortgage payments do not repay the capital. The advantage of this mortgage is that you have lower monthly mortgage payments. The disadvantage is that the outstanding debt remains constant. So, if you borrow £150,000 and only make interest payments for 25 years, you will owe £150,000 at the end of that 25 years.
However, most lenders will allow borrowers to make overpayments (usually up to 10% of your mortgage balance per annum), which allows you to repay the mortgage at a level you can afford.
You may also be required to show how you plan to repay the mortgage at the end of the term. For most people, that would mean making regular monthly contributions into an ISA.
If you are very disciplined with money, this is a viable mortgage option. The overpayments are not compulsory; nor

is the amount you pay into your ISA. But you have to do these things if you ever want to be mortgage-free.

Fixed-rate mortgages vs standard-variable-rate mortgages

With standard-variable-rate mortgages the interest you pay on your monthly mortgage payments can go up or down, depending on where your mortgage lender decides to set its standard variable rate. In other words, you are at the mercy of your mortgage provider. I would not recommend this type of mortgage.

With fixed-rate mortgages, the interest rate is fixed for a set period of time. The interest rate is usually fixed for two or five years. You can get ten-year fixed-rate mortgages too, but they are pretty uncommon. The key advantage of a fixed-rate mortgage is certainty, which makes it much easier to budget. The most common fixed-rate mortgage is a two-year fixed. But you should be wary of this. As a first-time buyer, mortgage lenders tend to be very generous in terms of fees they charge. When you remortgage, expect to pay, for example, an arrangement fee of up to £2,000. As such, most first-time buyers should opt for a five-year fixed deal. Unless you are completely sure you will never move, in which case consider a 10-year deal. In terms of interest rates, the longer the rate is fixed, the higher the interest you should expect to pay.

Other types of mortgages

Tracker mortgages track the Bank of England's base rate. So, for example, if the base rate was 1%, your mortgage term may stipulate "base rate + 1.25%", making your monthly repayments 2.25%. Needless to say, your monthly payments would vary in accordance with base rate changes.

Capped mortgages are similar to standard-variable-rate mortgages in that the interest you pay on your monthly mortgage payments can go up or down, depending on where your mortgage lender decides to set its standard variable rate. Where they differ is that there is an upper limit on the interest you can be charged. So, you benefit if interest rates fall, and are protected if they rise too much.

Offset mortgages link the borrower's mortgage account and savings account. Any savings you hold are offset against mortgage interest payments, so you only pay interest on your mortgage balance minus your savings balance. To give an example: if you have a mortgage of £200,000 and savings of £10,000, you would only pay interest on £190,000. Your savings do not reduce the amount you owe, but they do reduce the interest you pay. As your savings are reducing the amount of interest you pay, it should be possible to pay off your mortgage more quickly. But, unlike making overpayments, you can still withdraw your savings whenever you want. Plus the effective interest rate on your savings will be a market beater: if you are paying 4% on your mortgage, that is effectively what you are receiving on your savings in your offset account. If you're financially savvy, offset mortgages might be a good option.

100% mortgages. I have included these as I am often asked about them. But I do not recommend them for anyone, unless kamikaze is your thing. The 100% mortgage became popular in the housing boom of the early 2000s. In fact, remarkably, some lenders offered 125% mortgages, assuming house price rises would never stop. One such lender was Northern Rock - it was taken into public ownership in 2008, as an alternative to insolvency. 100% mortgages were withdrawn from the market in 2008 and seemed to have gone the way of the dodo. However, in 2015 the latest wave of 100% mortgages was born.

So, to state the obvious, with a 100% mortgage you do not need a deposit. But there are plenty of pitfalls. Firstly, there are currently just a few lenders offering such mortgages - that lack of competition usually means higher interest rates and fees. Secondly, there are a number of hoops you need to jump through. For example, you will probably need a family member to act as a guarantor. In simple terms, that person would need to pay the loan were you unable to. Some lenders will want a legal charge registered on the guarantor's home (i.e. their property will be secured against the loan too), which is not good. The lender can pursue the guarantor for any shortfall if the borrower has their home repossessed and sold. So, one mortgage, but two properties as security. Other lenders will ask for savings as security. But the savings are another family member's and this money is held for a set number of years in a savings account with the lender. Again, this is far from ideal.

100% mortgages helped fuel the 2008 financial crisis. Many homeowners were plunged into negative equity. (Negative equity is the worst-case scenario for a homeowner. It makes it very hard to sell the property and equally hard to remortgage, without paying punitive interest rates.)

The revamped 100% mortgages are similar, but worse. They are designed so the bank cannot lose. Instead, all the risk is transferred to the borrower (and the borrower's family). Yet the chance of falling into negative equity remains the same. I do not think any first-time buyer should consider a 100% mortgage.

Guarantor mortgages. This is any mortgage where a guarantor effectively underwrites the loan. In simple terms, you find someone (usually a family member) to agree to pay the loan if you cannot. The term "guarantor mortgage" is an umbrella term for any type of mortgage that is "guaranteed" by a third party. So, you could have a "guarantor repayment mortgage" or a "guarantor interest-only mortgage". Guarantor mortgages are used when it's the only way you are able to borrow what you require to buy the property. By having a guarantor you will be able to borrow more money. This is how it works: the guarantor will sign a legal agreement to make your repayments if you are unable. In addition, the lender either holds a legal charge on the guarantor's property, or they will ask the guarantor to put a lump sum into a savings account held by them. In terms of the former, technically the guarantor's property could be repossessed if you fall way behind on your payments. With the latter, the guarantor will be unable to withdraw this money for a set number of years.

Guarantors are usually family members. But some lenders will allow friends to act as guarantors too. Your guarantor will also need to:

- Be a property owner, usually outright or with substantial equity in the property.
- Be earning enough money to cover the mortgage payments if you're unable to make them.
- Have an excellent credit score. More on this later.
- Receive independent legal advice. This is because some lenders will need to see evidence of this before offering this mortgage. I fully support seeking legal advice, as there are risks involved.

As you will have noticed, guarantor mortgages and 100% mortgages have some similarities. However, with the former, there is less chance of falling into negative equity.

As such, I am more ambivalent with regards to guarantor mortgages. They definitely have their place, and may be suitable for some first-time buyers. In particular people with professional qualifications who are highly likely to see their salary rise considerably over time.

The mortgage term

This is the length of time the borrowing is required. The most common mortgage term for a first-time buyer is 25 years. This is important when calculating monthly payments on repayment mortgages.

Initially, a larger proportion of the monthly mortgage payments will be interest payments. But, as you gradually chip away at the outstanding capital, these interest payments will start to reduce and a larger proportion of your monthly payments will go towards paying off your mortgage.

The longer the mortgage term, the smaller your monthly payments. But, of course, the longer you owe money the more interest you will pay in total. To make monthly payments more manageable, some people opt for a longer mortgage term. This is fine provided you remember to reduce the term once you have a little more money (and are due to remortgage the property).

Stamp duty

Stamp Duty Land Tax (SDLT) is payable if you buy a property or land over a certain price in England and Northern Ireland. In Scotland you pay Land and Buildings Transaction Tax. In Wales you pay Land Transaction Tax.

The amount you pay depends on the price of the property, as it's a progressive tax. Fortunately there are special rates for first-time buyers. Here's how it works in England for first-time buyers:

- First-time buyers do not pay any stamp duty up to £300,000.
- Then, from between £300,001 to £500,000 you pay 5%.

If the property you are buying costs over £500,000, the balance above this amount is paid at the same rate as everyone else. Which is as follows:

Property value	SDLT rate
Up to £125,000	Zero
The next £125,000 (the portion from £125,001 to £250,000)	2%
The next £675,000 (the portion from £250,001 to £925,000)	5%
The next £575,000 (the portion from £925,001 to £1.5 million)	10%
The remaining amount (the portion above £1.5 million)	12%

So, effectively, first-time buyers pay 0% on the first £300,000, then 5% on the next £625,000, then 10% on everything between £925,001 to £1.5 million, and finally 12% on everything above £1.5 million. Although, I suspect, few first-time buyers will be affected by the highest rates.

Stamp duty examples (for a first-time buyer in England):

If you buy a house for £450,000, the SDLT you owe is calculated as follows:
- 0% on the first £300,000 = £0
- 5% on the next £150,000 = £7,500
- Total SDLT = £7,500

If you buy a house for £250,000, the SDLT you owe is calculated as follows:
- 0% on the first £250,000 = £0
- Total SDLT = £0

So, stamp duty can be a considerable tax and it's important to budget for this. It should be noted that this tax is paid on the day you legally acquire the property, and is unavoidable. Unless you buy a zero-carbon home.

Zero-carbon homes relief
Zero-carbon homes relief is a relief from stamp duty for new homes that meet a specified standard of energy efficiency. Since October 2007 all zero-carbon homes costing less than £500,000 are exempt from stamp duty. If the property costs more than £500,000, the total stamp duty bill is reduced by £15,000. The vendor of a new zero-carbon home must provide a certificate confirming that the home qualifies for the relief. Unfortunately, very few homes qualify as zero carbon. For more information, Google: "Zero carbon homes relief".

Mortgage fees

There are a multitude of additional fees you may have to pay. Some of these are completely inexplicable. But, I will do my best.

Mortgage-arrangement fee. This is a fee levied by the lender to access the mortgage product. You do not pay this until your purchase has been completed. Some lenders will allow you to add this to your mortgage. Typically these arrangement fees range between £0 and £3,000. Although, as a first-time buyer, you would hope not to pay a mortgage-arrangement fee. Always read the small print.

Booking fee. This one really niggles, as this is charged when you simply apply for a mortgage. It's not usually refundable, even if your property purchase doesn't materialise. Again, as a first-time buyer you can expect to avoid this. If not, it's usually less than £300.

Valuation fee. All mortgage providers will value the property you are planning on buying to ensure it's worth what you have offered. This helps protect both you and the lender. But, of course, it's you who picks up the tab. Expect to pay between £300 +VAT and £750 +VAT depending on the value of the property and the type of survey you commission. (More on the different types of surveys later.) Some lenders waive this fee for first-time buyers.

CHAPS. When your mortgage lender transfers the loan money to your solicitor they charge telegraphic transfer fee (this is sometimes known as CHAPS - Clearing House Automated Payment System). Expect to pay no more than £50.

Mortgage advisor. If you use a mortgage advisor you will need to pay them too. (More on mortgage advisors later.) Most charge a flat fee for their advice. Some do not charge a fee, but are paid a commission by their lender. If it's the former, expect to pay in the region of £500.

Higher lending charges. Higher lending charges are only levied on those who are putting down a very small deposit (and are rarely levied on first-time buyers). It is effectively an insurance against you not being able to pay the mortgage. Most people pay 1.5% of the property's value. But there have been cases where people have been quoted 8%.

Early repayment charges. As mentioned before, most lenders will allow borrowers to make overpayments, usually up to 10% of your mortgage balance per annum. However, if you want to repay the whole mortgage early, an early repayment charge will apply. These mainly come into effect if you want to repay within the fixed-rate period, and tend to be on a sliding scale. For example, if you have a five-year fixed-rate mortgage, you could expect to pay:

5% of the property value in year 1
4% of the property value in year 2
3% of the property value in year 3
2% of the property value in year 4
1% of the property value in year 5

So, if your outstanding mortgage was £250,000, here's how much the early repayment fee would be:
In year 1 it would be 5% of £250,000 = £12,500
In year 2 it would be 4% of £250,000 = £10,000
In year 3 it would be 3% of £250,000 = £7,500
In year 4 it would be 2% of £250,000 = £5,000
In year 5 it would be 1% of £250,000 = £2,500

This is, of course, just an example. Each lender will have their own criteria, and it's vital you are aware of this before agreeing to any mortgage.

Mortgage advisors

In the 1990s many predicted the death of the financial advisor. Direct Line's advertising suggested people should cut out the middleman; the idea being that this would save you money. Various financial institutions started offering "direct" products – you can buy ISAs, pensions and a myriad of other products online. But mortgage advisors survived and thrived. And with good reason. Finding a good mortgage advisor is like finding or good doctor or dentist. Except these guys help with your financial health. Post global financial crisis, the mortgage industry is now highly regulated - you need an expert to help you navigate these choppy waters.

The different types of mortgage advisors

Tied agents. Tied agents work for one company and sell their mortgage products. For example, HSBC will employ mortgage advisors, but they will only know about and sell HSBC's mortgage products. The only advantage of using a tied agent is if you bank with that company and have demonstrated, through your bank account, that you are financially competent. This may help you get your mortgage approved.

Independent Financial Advisors (IFAs). IFAs are, as the name suggests, independent. Independent mortgage advisors provide unbiased, impartial advice. They can scour the whole market for the best deals. I strongly suggest you use an Independent Financial Advisor. You are far more likely to get your mortgage approved and to get a lower interest rate on your loan. In addition, banks will invariably try to cross-sell other products, such as current accounts and insurance. IFAs tend not to do this.

Top tip: Estate agents sometimes suggest that you'll be more likely to be put forward as the "preferred buyer" if you use their financial advisor. This is illegal - so make sure they know you know. If this does happen, ask to speak to the manager and, if they persist, threaten to report them to the Financial Ombudsman Service.

Right, back to mortgage advisors. Another huge benefit of using a mortgage advisor is that they will do all the paperwork. You will have to provide supporting evidence, but you won't have to fill out any forms. Once you have decided the best mortgage for you, the process should take no more than 30 minutes on the phone.

The next advantage is that a good mortgage advisor will hugely improve the chance of your mortgage being approved. A raft of new rules, introduced by the Financial Conduct Authority, have led to ever-tightening mortgage-lending criteria. This has meant customers who, in the past, may have been granted a loan, are now being rejected – and everyone is facing closer financial scrutiny. And the way each lender interprets these rules is nuanced. Mortgage advisors will know which lender is most likely to approve your application based on your individual circumstances. This can save a huge amount of legwork, and can make the process far less stressful.

If your mortgage requirements are straightforward – for example, you're borrowing a low multiple of your income – you may not *need* to use a mortgage advisor. However, if your needs are more complicated – for example, you're self employed or want to borrow towards the upper end of the lending scale (i.e. 4½ times your salary) – your mortgage could prove far harder to arrange. And even if it's going to be simple to arrange, I would still suggest you use a mortgage advisor. They are far more likely to secure you the best interest rate.

The advice is definitely worth paying for: getting the best mortgage can save you tens of thousands of pounds in interest. Mortgage advisors tend to charge either a fixed fee or a percentage of the loan. I always choose the former, but that's just my personal preference. The last time I used a mortgage advisor they charged me £400. It was money well spent. Moreover, a good mortgage advisor will not only consider your position today but will take into account future plans and objectives.

How to find the best mortgage advisor
Almost 70% of home loans are arranged by mortgage advisors, but that doesn't mean everyone who uses an advisor is getting the best deal. First off, ask your friends and family for recommendations. If you still draw a blank, look at Google Reviews and their other online ratings (e.g. Trustpilot). If you have the time, try to meet with three in person. Did they truly listen to you and fully understand your financial position and future goals? If the answer is yes, you have probably found the right IFA for you. I have used the same, excellent, IFA for years. They are contacts well worth nurturing.

Top tip: Before you start looking for a property, you should obtain a "**mortgage in principle**". This is a certificate issued by a lender that says, in principle, how much money they would be willing to lend you. The key advantage of this is that you suddenly become a more viable buyer. This means your offer is more likely to be accepted. Note: a mortgage in principle is normally valid for between 60 and 90 days. But, assuming your circumstances haven't changed, you can be pretty confident the same offer will be made again. Do not reapply too often, as doing so could damage your credit score. (More on credit scores later.)

What evidence do lenders need

As part of the mortgage-approval process, most lenders will require you to provide the following:

- Your passport (either an original or a certified copy).
- A utility bill in your name at your home address dated in the last two months.
- Last three months' payslips.
- Last two years' P60s.
- Last three months' bank statements across all accounts.
- Last three months' savings account statements.

This list is not definitive, as each lender's requirements will differ. In addition, if you are self-employed, you may also be expected to provide such things as:

- Last three years tax calculations.
- Last three years' tax overviews.

You will also be asked to provide information about your current expenditure and other financial commitments. In particular, lenders will want to know about any credit-card debt. You really need to have a zero balance on all of your credit cards.

Tidy up your finances

If you are saving for a deposit, now is the time to tidy up your finances. As I mentioned before, lenders will look carefully at your expenditure. Lenders will require a household budget, so it's worth pulling this information together. You should also consider jettisoning some unnecessary costs, such as gym membership. In fact, shop around for anything you can that will reduce your monthly outgoings. Move to a SIM-only mobile phone deal, for example.

Your credit score
Having a good credit score is vital if you want your mortgage application approved. Each adult's credit score is created by the Credit Reference Agencies. Most credit scores range from 300 to 850 - the higher your score the better. The Credit Reference Agencies are private companies. The three main ones in the UK are Equifax, Experian and TransUnion. Between them, they collect millions of pieces of information each month and gradually, over a period of time, each person's credit score is ascertained. These are the main sources of their information:

- **Electoral-roll data**. This is publicly available information that includes people's names and addresses. Make sure you are on the electoral roll for the property at which you currently reside.
- **Court records**. These include County Court Judgments (CCJs), decrees, Individual Voluntary Arrangements (IVAs), bankruptcies and other court debt orders. These records are used by lenders to assess whether you've had debt problems in the past. If this is part of your credit history, tell your mortgage advisor in advance as there are some lenders who will be lenient, especially if there were mitigating circumstances.
- **Credit applications at addresses linked to you**. Each time you apply for credit (for example, when you get a mobile-phone contract) this information is put on

your file. It includes all the past addresses you've been linked to. Most large gas and electricity firms do credit checks too. This data is also added to your file.

- **Account data**. The banks, building societies, utility companies and other organisations share details of your account behaviour over the last six years. Account behaviour could include loans, store cards, mobile-phone-contract payments, utility bill payments, etc. If you have defaulted on any of these, your credit score will be negatively affected. There have been numerous stories of people missing a single payment subsequently being rejected for a mortgage. This happens more when people have moved and have failed to provide a forwarding address.

If you apply for a mortgage and your credit score is poor, you will be rejected. That is the harsh truth. You should start managing your credit file at least a year before you apply for your first mortgage. But, in truth, most people don't know their own credit score. So, first up, you can check your credit score online. Experian and Equifax, for example, allow you to do this for free. But, beware; the free month-long trials are used as loss leaders – make sure you cancel your subscription once you've checked your score.

Top tip: If you spot anything that's incorrect on your report, you can apply to have it removed.

How to improve your credit score
If you find you have a poor credit score, you will need to work to improve it. This can take some time, so start now. Aside from making sure you are on the electoral roll, here are some other things you should do:

- **Credit-card debt.** If you have credit-card debt, you need to pay this off as soon as possible. You then need to get into the habit of paying off your credit-card bill in full every month.
- **Creating credit history**. Oddly, some people are declined mortgages as they have too little credit history. So, if that's you, you need to build your credit score. The best way to do this is to get a credit card and use it every month for a year. But you have to pay your credit-card bill in full every month. Paying a monthly mobile-phone bill will help too.
- **Cancel credit cards that you don't use**. Some lenders don't like that fact the people with multiple credit cards have access to instant [high-interest] cash without having to pass additional credit checks.
- **Check all the addresses on your file**. One of the issues with "going paperless" is that it's easier to forget to change your address when you move. Even having your mobile contract registered at an old address can lead to a mortgage being declined. If there is anything on your credit file registered to an old address, get this amended.
- **Credit cards are not ATMs**. Under no circumstance should you withdraw cash from your credit card. It will be noted on your file and earmarks you as profligate.
- **Remember the records only go back six years**. If you have anything ugly on your file, such as County Court Judgments (CCJs), you may be able to wait it out. Check the date and see if that's a possible option.

- **Don't get held back by your ex**. Close any joint bank accounts, credit cards, etc. held with your ex-partner. Also, you can write to the credit agencies and ask them to delink you. Otherwise you are at risk of their poor credit history dragging you down too.
- **Don't use your overdraft**. This will not only improve your credit rating, it will also look better on your application. Remember, lenders will want to see three months' worth of bank statements.
- **Prioritise your mortgage application**. Try not to apply for any credit in the six months running up to your mortgage application. Each time you do, it will get added to your file. Applying for too much credit makes you look somewhat desperate. Please note: credit applications only stay on your file for a year.
- **Never take out a payday loan**. Most lenders will reject your application out of hand as they will consider you unable to manage basic finances.

In summary, the banks' lending criteria seem to change on a weekly basis. But the fundamentals remain the same: your income, credit score, deposit and financial situation are key. Put your financial house in order and you'll have a much better chance of having your mortgage application approved.

The impact of student loans

Tuition fees were introduced by the Labour Government in autumn 1998. At the time, they were just £1,000 a year. However, since then they have been tripled twice: once in 2006 (to £3,000) and again in 2012 (to £9,000). At the time of writing, the current cap is £9,250 per annum. And, although it's a cap, almost all universities charge the maximum amount. Of course, there are maintenance loans too, which are up to a maximum of £11,672 (if you're living away from home in London). These figures change every year, so check for up-to-date information.

The tripling of tuition fees to £9,000 in 2012 at first glance looks utterly galling. However, the Government did sugar the pill: they raised the repayment income threshold. Currently, after graduating, no one has to pay back any money until they are earning over £25,725. Thereafter, repayments are calculated at 9%. If you don't pay it all off in 30 years, the remaining debt is written off.

Here's a worked example (based on someone who took out a student loan from 2012 onwards):

Salary	Amount of salary from which 9% will be deducted	Monthly repayment
£30,000.00	£4,275.00	£32.06
£35,000.00	£9,275.00	£69.56
£40,000.00	£14,275.00	£107.06
£45,000.00	£19,275.00	£144.56
£50,000.00	£24,275.00	£182.06
£55,000.00	£29,275.00	£219.56
£60,000.00	£34,275.00	£257.06

The impact of student loans on mortgage applications
The first thing to know is that student loans do not count as debt. Nor do they affect your credit score. (The only exception to this is borrowers who took out their loans before

1998 and defaulted on a payment.) Moreover, as you can see from the example above, the total amount you borrowed as a student does not affect your mandatory repayment obligations. What affects your repayment amount is how much you earn. So, it's probably better to view these payments as a tax on success. For example, if you end up earning £100,000, your monthly repayments would be £557.06. But, firstly, you can afford them. And, secondly, your success would almost certainly have been, at least in part, due to your university education. Would you really begrudge making these payments? I don't think so.

But I digress. When you apply for a mortgage, you do not have to provide information about your outstanding student loans. So, in that regard, having considerable student debt will not count against you. However, you do have to provide details of your monthly expenditure commitments (plus three months of bank statements). So, when checking the affordability of the mortgage, this will be taken into account.

Student-loan debt vs. mortgage debt

Like a mortgage, student loans accrue interest. The rate of interest is based on the Retail Price Index (RPI) rate of inflation. There are two measures of inflation: the Retail Price Index (RPI) and the Consumer Price Index (CPI). The only thing you need to know is that the RPI is almost always the higher measure of inflation. In fact, with the exception of 2009, it has been for the last 20 years. What you do need to know is the level of interest on your student loan. Here's how it's calculated (based on someone who took out a student loan from 2012 onwards):

- If you earn £25,725 or less you pay just the RPI rate of inflation.

- If you earn between £25,725 and £46,305 you pay RPI plus an interest rate that will gradually rise from RPI to RPI + 3% the more you earn
- If you earn over £46,305 you pay just the RPI rate of inflation + 3%.

The RPI rate is set every September using the rate from March of the same year. In March 2018 the RPI rate of inflation was 3.3%, so from September 2018 to August 2019 the interest on student loan debt will be 6.3% (or 3.3% for those earning under £25,725).

This is important to know, because this will almost certainly be more expensive than mortgage debt. So, it may seem like a better option to try to pay this off first. However, a recent report by The Institute for Fiscal Studies (IFS) concluded that three-quarters of graduates will never clear their student debt. Given that any outstanding debt is written off after 30 years (and that you can't get your property repossessed if you miss a student loan payment), it may, perversely, be better to try to clear your cheaper mortgage debt first.

Top tip: If you are overpaying on your student loan repayments, you should probably stop doing so four months before you apply for a mortgage. Instead pay the minimum monthly amount. This will make your mortgage payments look more affordable.

Note: If you started studying before 1 September 2012 the figures are different. For example, you need to start repaying your loans when you earn more than £17,775. And, for these loans, the interest is calculated at the RPI rate of inflation.

Mortgage underwriters

The mortgage underwriter, who will be an employee of your prospective lender, is the person responsible for approving or disapproving your mortgage application. The underwriter will review your application form and the accompanying documentation and determine whether you have the capacity to repay the mortgage loan. They are also interested in the type of property, as some are seen as higher risk than others. Finally, they need to ensure that the lending falls within the requirements of their institution and current Government regulations. A good mortgage advisor should preempt any possible issues the underwriter may have. As such, the mortgage underwriter will, hopefully, rubber stamp your application. However, underwriters will often ask for additional information. Make sure you supply this in a timely manner. If your application is rejected, you can ask why and you can appeal this decision.

Budgeting

Convincing the underwriter is one thing. You also need to be sure yourself - can you afford to be a homeowner? If you are currently living at home (and therefore being subsidised by your parents), the cost of running your own home may come as a shock. Here are the things most homeowners have to pay for:

- The mortgage
- Electricity
- Gas
- Water
- Council tax
- Broadband
- Phone line

- TV licence
- Buildings insurance
- Contents insurance
- Repairs/redecoration
- White goods
- Furnishings
- Gardening costs
- Ground rent (leasehold properties)
- Service charges (leasehold properties)

Moreover, homeowners are sometimes hit with large unexpected bills, such as replacing the boiler. Squirrelling away an emergency fund is essential.

Part 2 - Government help for first-time buyers

Over the years, various Governments have put schemes in place to help first-time buyers. These are ever-changing, so definitely do your own online research to check all the schemes detailed below are still running in the described format. Google: "Government help for first-time buyers" or click on this link: https://www.helptobuy.gov.uk/

Help to Buy - Shared Ownership

This scheme has been set up in conjunction with Housing Associations. (Housing Associations are non-profit organisations that rent properties to people on low incomes or with particular needs.) Effectively, Shared Ownership offers prospective buyers the chance to buy a share of a property – the Housing Association owns the rest. Buyers can purchase between 25% and 75% of the property's value. Rent is then payable on the remaining portion. The scheme includes newly-built properties or ones made available through resale programmes from Housing Associations. Shared Ownership is not open to everyone, but the allowances are pretty generous. In England your household income needs to be less than £80,000 a year (in London this rises to £90,000). Also, you must be one of the following:

- A first-time buyer.
- Someone who used to be a homeowner, but who no longer owns a property.
- An existing shared owner who wants to move.

The upsides of Shared Ownership:

- Shared ownership allows people on very modest incomes to become homeowners – in part at least. It also allows you to increase your ownership all the way to 100%. This is through a process called "staircasing", whereby you have the right to raise your equity stake.

- The rent you pay on the portion of the property you don't own is capped. Each Housing Association will calculate rent payments in different ways. But, typically, the initial rent will be based on a sum equivalent to 3% of the outstanding equity retained by the Housing Association. The rent may then increase annually in line with increases to the RPI (Retail Price Index) rate of inflation.

- Another consideration is that Housing Associations are non-profit organisations that rent properties to people on low incomes. They were not set up as profit maximisers. As such, they are normally reasonable landlords.

The downsides of Shared Ownership:

- When you can afford to raise your stake, you have to pay the "current market value" for the additional percentage you want to buy. In addition, some people have complained of high administration fees each time they have tried to "staircase".

- All Shared Ownership properties are leasehold. (More on leasehold properties later.) Worse still, a Shared-Ownership lease does not qualify for the right to purchase the freehold. This is a right that all other leaseholders enjoy as a result of the Leasehold Reform Act 1967. Another thing to consider is that a Shared-Ownership leaseholder only qualifies for the statutory right to extend their lease if they have "staircased" up to 100% ownership. However, some landlords have their own policy of allowing lease extension where there is less than 100% ownership. Make sure your conveyancing solicitor investigates this thoroughly and that you are aware of the possible implications.

- On top of rent, you will have to pay maintenance fees, annual service charges and a share of the buildings insurance. Ground rent may also be payable. Additionally, freeholder permission will have to be obtained should you want to undertake any major renovations. On top of this, leaseholders may face other restrictions, such as not owning pets. Again, these are worth investigating before committing.

Is Shared Ownership a good option for first-time buyers?
If you can afford to buy a property outright, definitely not. However, if you're likely to see your salary rise, it's a great way for young people to get onto the property ladder.
To buy a home through a Shared Ownership scheme, contact the Help to Buy agent in the area you want to live. Click on this link to find the right Help to Buy agent:
https://www.helptobuy.gov.uk/equity-loan/find-helptobuy-agent/

Shared Ownership - for older people
If you're aged 55 or over, and are struggling to afford to buy your own home, you can buy up to 75% of your home through the Older People's Shared Ownership (OPSO) scheme. Once you own 75% you won't pay rent on the rest.

Shared Ownership - for disabled people
You can apply for a scheme called "Home ownership for people with long-term disabilities (HOLD)" if other "Help to

Buy - Shared Ownership" scheme properties don't meet your needs. For example, if you need a ground-floor property.

Help to Buy - Equity Loan Scheme
The Equity Loan Scheme allows buyers to borrow more money to get onto the property ladder. The Government lends you up to 20% of the cost of your newly-built home (in Greater London, the Government will lend you up to 40%). You will need at least a 5% cash deposit – the rest being made up by a commercial mortgage of up to 75% of the purchase price. The property must cost no more than £600,000.

The Government loan is interest-free for the first five years of you owning the property – although a monthly management fee of £1 is levied during the time of the loan. After five years the interest rate rises to 1.75%. Thereafter, it will rise each year by the increase (if any) in the Retail Prices Index (RPI) plus 1%. The loan itself is repayable after 25 years or on the sale of the property – whichever is earlier.

All Equity Loan properties are listed online by region. For a full list, click on this link:
https://www.helptobuy.gov.uk/equity-loan/find-helptobuy-agent/

What's the catch?
- Following the purchase you can make voluntary part repayments of the Equity Loan at the "prevailing market value" – in other words, if your property has risen by 20% in value, the loan will have too.
- If you sell your home, you must repay the same percentage of the proceeds of the sale to the Government as the initial equity loan (i.e. if you received an equity loan for 15% of the purchase price

of your home, you must repay 15% of the proceeds of the future sale).

Given the "catches" listed above, anyone using this scheme needs to be on the ball. At first glance, it makes no sense to pay off the Government loan before your commercial loan – especially in the first five years when it's interest-free. However, perversely, this might not be the case. If prices are rising rapidly, paying down the equity loan first could be the best option.

Other legalities:

- You won't be able to sublet this home and you must not own any other property at the time of purchase.
- For some unknown reason, the Equity Loan scheme requires that the owner has a main mortgage of at least 25% of the purchase price. If anyone can tell me why, I would love to know.
- Buyers cannot use the scheme if they require a main mortgage that's more than 4½ times their household income.

Please note: This scheme is available in England only. The Scottish Government, Welsh Government and Northern Ireland Housing Executive run similar schemes, which are definitely worth investigating.

Top tip: The government have published a remarkably helpful and comprehensive guide to their Equity Loan Scheme. Here's the link: https://www.helptobuy.gov.uk/wp-content/uploads/Help-to-Buy-Buyers-Guide-Feb-2018-FINAL.pdf

Right to Buy (a council property)

The Right to Buy was launched by the Conservative Government in 1980. Since then, over 1.5 million people have purchased their properties via this scheme. Although not without its critics, it did, for a time, help Britain become a "nation of homeowners".

Here's how it works:

- If you have been a council tenant for three years, you may have the right to buy your property at a discounted rate. This also applies to other public-sector tenants (e.g. armed services or NHS foundations).
- The maximum discount is: £110,500 in London, £82,800 in rest of England and £24,000 in Northern Ireland. The amount of the discount will depend on factors including: how long you have been a tenant, the type of property and the current value of the property. There's an online calculator that helps you work out your potential discount: https://righttobuy.gov.uk/right-to-buy-calculator/
- Note: many people are put off Right to Buy because they don't have a deposit. But, neatly, most lenders will view the discount as your deposit. Result!
- However, you will still need to raise a mortgage for the remaining amount you need. For most people, this will mean proving your income, etc.
- The value of the property will be estimated when you apply. To do this and to apply, follow this link: https://www.gov.uk/right-to-buy-buying-your-council-home
- You will then receive an offer letter (called a Section 125 Notice). This will include the valuation, discount amount, purchase price, structural problems (if any exist) and the terms and conditions of the sale. Read this carefully.

- If you are happy with the offer, you can then proceed onto the purchase.
- Once the purchase has been completed, you need to live in this property for at least five years. If you don't, you will have to pay back some or all of the discount you received. Here are the amounts you would need to pay back:
  - 100% of the discount in the first year.
  - 80% of the discount in the second year.
  - 60% of the discount in the third year.
  - 40% of the discount in the fourth year.
  - 20% of the discount in the fifth year.

If you are a council tenant and you are able, I urge you to invoke your Right to Buy. It's one of the best ways onto the property ladder. For further details, follow this link: https://www.gov.uk/right-to-buy-buying-your-council-home

Note: In Northern Ireland this scheme is known as the House Sales Scheme and is open to tenants renting from a housing association or the Northern Ireland Housing Executive.
The Right to Acquire (as it was known) in Wales ended in January 2019.

Lifetime (Individual Savings Account) ISA
See "Part 1 - Financing your first property purchase".

Rent to buy/rent to own
These are little-known schemes that are supposed to help first-time buyers get onto the property ladder. Rent to own is available in England, Scotland and Northern Ireland. Rent to buy is a similar scheme for people living in Wales.
I will provide further details below, but I want to be up front: I am highly sceptical about these schemes. Rent-to-buy

properties are provided by Housing Associations, but there are virtually no rent-to-buy properties available. Also, currently, rent to buy is only available for new-build properties. Here's how **rent to buy** works:

- To be eligible for a rent-to-buy scheme your household income must be £60,000 or less. A household is defined as one person, or a couple or you and a friend. It's only open to first-time buyers, or to people who used to own their own home, but who can no longer afford to buy a property on the open market. You will need to have a good credit history too. Moreover, each Housing Association may have their own additional criteria - many favour existing housing association tenants and council tenants.

- Once you find a rent-to-buy property (in England, Scotland or Northern Ireland), you will be able to rent this property at approximately 80% of the market rate for up to five years (although this will vary from property to property). During that period you have the option to buy either the entire property or a percentage of the property under the Shared Ownership scheme. There is no central list of eligible properties in England and Scotland. Participating Housing Association properties in Northern Ireland can be found here: https://www.co-ownership.org/

With **rent to own**, again you rent the property for up to five years. You do not get a rent reduction. Instead, if you apply to buy the property, you will receive a 25% rebate on the rent you've paid, plus 50% of any increase in the property's value since you started renting it. This money can then be used as a deposit against this property purchase. Participating landlords in Wales can be found here: https://gov.wales/rent-own-wales-participating-landlords

In theory, these schemes are quite appealing. But the lack of eligible properties is a huge negative.

Part 3 - Finding the right property for you

Location - what to look for

Property hunting can be tremendous fun. It can also be a massive waste of time and energy. To avoid it being the latter, try to narrow down your search area. Location, of course, is key. Here are some factors that you need to consider when deciding where to live:

- **School catchment areas**. For many people this will be a prerequisite. Living within a good school's catchment area can hugely improve your children's life chances. However, properties in such locations tend to attract a premium. For school performance tables, click on this link: www.compare-school-performance.service.gov.uk. Of course the league tables don't tell the full picture. Ofsted reports are worth reading and there's no substitute for visiting a school.

- **Transport**. Being close to a train or tube station, or bus or tram stops, is not only very handy, it will also help if you ever come to sell. Also, if you need to commute to work, the length of that commute can hugely affect your quality of life. The type of commute makes a big difference too. A half-empty reliable train journey is infinitely more pleasant than a rush-hour sardine-like tube journey. It's well worth trying the commute out in advance.

- **Do you feel safe?** It's vital you feel safe where you live. Getting the feel for an area doesn't take too long: are children playing on the street/in local parks, are people going for a walk, is there litter or graffiti? Consider when the lights go down too. Would you be happy to walk home after the hours of darkness? If the answer is "no" you may need a rethink. Of course, the perception of crime in the UK is usually worse than the reality. It is worth checking out local crime statistics though. Google: "crime statistics by postcode" to find a variety of websites offering this information for free. Also, www.police.uk is another good source of information.

- **Regeneration plans for the area**. If there is considerable building work planned in the area this may be very good in the long run, especially if these plans include improved transportation. But, short term, you may have to put up with noise, unsightly incomplete buildings and dust. You can find out what's being planned by visiting the Government's planning portal: www.planningportal.co.uk/

- **Up-and-coming areas**. If you can't afford where you would ideally like to live, look close by. Often grotty areas that adjoin smarter areas benefit from a spillover effect: gradually they gentrify. Provided that's not to the detriment of the local community, that's no bad thing. Look out for lots of scaffolding and skips. They are a sure sign of better times to come.

- **Mobile-phone reception**. Most people rely on their mobile phones, so having a poor reception is far from ideal. In fact, 4G (and now 5G) in some areas is a mandatory requirement. Check your phone when viewing any properties.

- **WiFi**. This is another essential, especially if you work from home or want to stream movies/television. Uswitch have a neat tool that allows you to check

broadband speeds by postcode:
www.uswitch.com/broadband/postcode_checker/

- **Local amenities.** It's important to have access to such things as shops, restaurants, sports clubs, libraries, a doctor's surgery, cycle lanes, pubs, a Post Office and places of worship. Moreover, such amenities help give rise to stronger communities. And that's often the difference between a property and a place called home.
- **Sports venues.** If you are close to any of these, you may need to be prepared for gridlock on match days. The same goes for any other large-scale entertainment venues. Sometimes this will be a regular occurrence; sometimes it will be less frequent. Glastonbury, for example, is pretty quiet for 360 (ish) days of the year.
- **Flood risks**. If the area has been subject to flooding in the past, you may find it difficult to insure your home. And, if you can find insurance, you may need to pay a premium. Of course, insurance is one thing: arriving home to a flooded property is another. That's most homeowner's worst nightmare. The Government publishes flood maps. Click on this link to view them: https://flood-map-for-planning.service.gov.uk/
- **Roads**. Being near to good road links is great; being blighted by traffic, noise and pollution isn't. In more rural locations, good road links are vital. If you're a city dweller, roads are often more of a nuisance. It's worth looking at air-pollution data too. You can find this here: www.apis.ac.uk/

- **Access to green (or blue) space**. This is especially important if the property is garden-less. Being close to a common or park is a big plus, as is being close to a river, lake or the sea (provided the property isn't at risk of being flooded).
- **Electric pylons.** These are unsightly and can emit annoying background noise. This may be of no concern to you, but it might put off future buyers if you ever decide to sell. Plus there is plenty of evidence that nearby pylons reduce property prices.
- **Coastal erosion**. This, of course, will not affect too many people. But it may do in the future. With sea levels highly likely to rise over the coming decades, it is worth paying close attention to possible future issues. The Government publishes coastal erosion maps: https://www.gov.uk/check-coastal-erosion-management-in-your-area

Once you have narrowed down your search area, it's time to consider the type of property that's right for you. Even if you're pretty sure you know what you're looking for, I urge you to be open-minded. Sometimes in life we don't know what we want until it's in front of our eyes.

Walking the streets
Researching an area online is a good starting point - thanks to Google Streetview, you can even take a virtual tour. However, there is no substitute for walking the streets. That's how you'll find hidden gems.

Different types of properties

- **Detached houses**. As their name suggests, these properties stand alone and are surrounded by their own land. While often being the most expensive to maintain and heat, they benefit from enhanced privacy.
- **Semi-detached houses**. This is when two properties are conjoined. You will share some maintenance costs with your neighbour. But you may hear them more too.
- **Terraced houses**. There are over 14 million terraced houses across the country. Some sell for tens of thousands of pounds; others tens of millions. It all depends on the location and size. Typically these are located in cities or past industrial towns and villages. They tend to be reasonably inexpensive to maintain and heat, depending on their age and condition.
- **End-of-terrace houses**. These properties suffer from what is known as a "cold wall". In older properties, these cold walls can cause countless issues such as damp and much-increased heating costs. I would avoid such properties, unless this wall has been repointed externally and insulated internally.
- **Flats**. These are any property that forms part of a larger property. Flats are the largest growing type of property. Large city-centre developments have fuelled this growth. Flats are often leasehold and subject to ground rent and service-charge costs. More on these later.
- **Conversion flats**. Many larger houses across the country have been converted into flats. All such work is overseen by Building Control, who assure the work

has met a certain standard. There was far less scrutiny in days gone by: beware of older conversions.

- **Purpose-built flats**. Unlike conversion flats, these have been designed and built as flats.
- **Studio flats**. Studio flats have only one main room: a living room that doubles up as a bedroom. More often than not, this room will incorporate a kitchen area too. Studio flats are mainly located within city centres.
- **Split-level flat**. This refers to any flat that has more than one floor. For example, a conversion flat set over two floors.
- **Maisonettes**. These are flats with their own external front door. These are less common. Most were built during the Victorian era.
- **Apartments**. According to the dictionary, an apartment is, "a flat, typically one that is well appointed or used for holidays". So, when you see the word "apartment" in an estate agent's property blurb, this is to make the property sound more salubrious.
- **Bungalows**. The word bungalow comes from the Hindi "bangala", which was a type of building originally developed in the Bengal region of the Indian subcontinent. A bungalow today is a property, normally detached, that is either single-story or has a second story built into a sloping roof. Bungalows have been much derided in the property world (at least in the UK), and have lagged behind the rest in terms of price rises. However, many come with large-ish plots of land and offer development potential.

- **Cottages**. Although the strict definition of a cottage is a small house, usually in the country, they are so much more than that. Their association with agricultural workers, fishermen and village life means they will long reside in many people's hearts. Cottages were built with thick walls, small windows and low ceilings to help withstand bitterly cold winters. Some are thatched too. The impracticalities of owning a cottage should not be ignored. Thatched roofs need to be completely re-thatched every 30 years. And thick stone walls offer little in terms of insulation.

New-build properties

One of the main advantages of buying a new-build property is that they invariably come with a warranty. The warranty (which is similar to insurance) is paid for by the builder and protects the home buyer. The three main providers are of these warranties are: Local Authority Building Control, Premier Guarantee and the National House Building Council. The latter is the most common. Most building warranties last 10 years, but what is covered is split between 1-2 years and 3-10 years. In the first two years, you are covered for pretty much all defects. After that, you are only covered for structural issues such as foundations, chimneys and roofs. Each warranty will vary; you should always read the small print.

Note: If you buy "off plan" (more on that later) the warranty will normally cover your deposit against the firm going into administration. So, if the property is never built, you will get your deposit back.

Another advantage of new builds is that you can often specify the finish you want. This could include the kitchen, the bathroom and the colour of the walls. Also, the running costs should be less. Short term, there should be few repairs to undertake. And new builds tend to have excellent insulation and double (or triple) glazing and efficient heating systems. This reduces your carbon footprint too.

New builds come with some negatives too:

- The developer's premium. New builds are often expensive, as the developer needs to make a profit.
- Beware of the show home. Show homes are designed to look spacious. They are usually in the best part of the development and are often the brightest. Moreover, they tend to be dressed with expensive trinkets and empty of the normal clutter of life (such as ironing boards and vacuum cleaners). Some developers also remove the internal doors and install furniture that's 75% of its normal size. Try to look beyond the razzmatazz; imagine living there day-to-day.
- Lack of local amenities. Some developments, especially out-of-town developments, lack basic amenities such as transport links and shops.
- Lack of community. Communities take time to grow; they are often lacking where new builds are concerned.
- Soulless. Many new builds lack character. Row upon row of identical properties isn't exactly inspiring.

New-build top tip

Pay a new-build surveyor to inspect the property. They will compile a snagging list for the developer to work through before you move in. Expect to pay between £300 and £1,000 for this, depending on the size of the property. This is money well spent, given that it's thought that most new-build properties have over 100 small defects (and some will have major defects too). Google "snagging survey" to find a new-build surveyor.

Buying off-plan

This is when you purchase a property that has yet to be built. This does require a leap of faith, as you will be buying based on architectural plans and an artist's impression of the completed property. Buying off-plan usually allows you to choose your own finish - for example, kitchen units, tiles and the colour of the paint. In addition, some developers offer a discount if you buy off-plan. Here are the main differences between buying off-plan and buying a property that has already been built:

- If you find an off-plan property you would like to buy, you can reserve this property for a nominal sum, often in the region of £1,000. But do not do this unless you have a mortgage in principle agreed.

- Once the property has been built, you will need to pay the deposit (usually around 10% of the agreed purchase price) and exchange contracts. Most developers expect the exchange of contracts to happen within 28 days. This means you have to get a valuation/survey completed by your lender and they have to agree to lend you the amount you require. If your lender does not agree with the valuation, you are at risk of losing your reservation fee.

- Most banks and building societies will require you to complete on the property within six months. Some will extend this period; others will expect you to re-apply for a mortgage. So, you need to get an accurate time-frame on the likely date the property will be finished. Most developers will provide prospective purchasers two dates: the expected date the property will be ready and the "long stop" date. The latter is the last date by which the developer has to have finished the property. If they miss this date, you are no longer contractually obliged to buy the property. Most developers will try to keep existing buyers lined up, often by offering discounts or other incentives. If you do have to re-apply for a mortgage there may be some hidden traps: if the lender deems that property prices have fallen, they may no longer be willing to lend you the money you require. This could cause you significant problems, as you have signed a legally-binding contract to buy the property. So, if you do have to pull out, expect to lose your deposit at a minimum.

- Some lenders may require two valuations: one before the property is finished and one when it is finished. As above, if the latter is a lower amount this may cause you problems. If this happens, here are your options:
  - o Make up the shortfall yourself.
  - o Renegotiate with the developer.
  - o Challenge the valuation.

Buying off-plan top tips
- Before you exchange contracts, ask your solicitor to add a get-out clause to the contract. If you are unable to raise the money at the point of completion despite making "reasonable efforts" to do so, you should be able to walk away without losing your deposit.
- Try to find a solicitor specialising in off-plan properties. Do not use the developer's solicitor. And

ask them the following questions (and make sure you are happy with the answers):

- o Is there planning consent for the development?
- o What happens if the developer goes bust before the development is finished?
- o What is included in the price? Sometimes there is a shopping list of "add ons" that add up.
- o Is the property freehold or leasehold? (More on freeholds and leaseholds later.)
- o If it is leasehold, what are the ground rent and service charges? And, how do these change year-on-year?
- o Are there different phases to the development? If you are phase one of a four-phase development, you could be surrounded by a building site for years.

Pre-owned properties

In the UK we're spoilt for choice. The most common period properties are Victorian; this is no surprise given the reign of Queen Victoria (1837 to 1901). There are also Tudor (1485–1603), Georgian (1714-1830), and Edwardian (1901-1910) properties. In fact, the oldest continuously occupied private home in England is Saltford Manor in Somerset. It was built before 1150. Talking of which, there are thought to be 500,000 listed properties in the UK too. And that's just the historic buildings. In the 20th century, house building peaked at 350,000 a year in the mid 1930s - this was the era of urban sprawl and the rise of the semi-detached property. In the 1950s, as Britain recovered from the war, there was a boom in local authority homes, with over 250,000 being built a year. The green belt was introduced then too. The 1960s heralded the era of the tower block, many of which have now been condemned and demolished. The 1970s wasn't much better: Artex ceilings, featureless facades and pebbledash were all in abundance. The quality of properties being built definitely started to improve in the 1990s. But so did the trend towards smaller rooms: indeed, according to recent research, new homes being built today are, on average, 32% smaller than they were in the 1970s.

For most people the question is period verses more modern. Period homes come with more features, but are more likely to suffer from such things as damp, woodworm and subsidence. The foundations of Georgian homes were often little more than a couple of bricks deep. On top of this, they will be more expensive to maintain. Period homes do have one big advantage: they are in limited supply (and they are not making any more). And, given that prices are determined by supply and demand, this may prove to be a significant long-term factor. Modern homes, on the other hand, may have less doorstep appeal, but they are often very comfortable places to live.

Ex-council properties

Some of the best value properties, in terms of space for your money, are ex-council. These properties range from terraced cottages to high-rise concrete monoliths, and everything in between. Here are some things to consider:

- What is the owner occupation rate? There are two reasons this is important. Firstly homeowners tend to take better care of their properties. And, secondly, some lenders will not lend if the ratio is too low (for example, less than 50%).

- Lenders are also sometimes reluctant to lend if the front doors of the property have access via a long communal balcony.
- Avoid large estates. Small is definitely beautiful in this instance. Look for small, low-rise, low-density developments in good locations. This should reduce service charges, especially if there isn't a lift. In addition, larger, more isolated estates are more likely to have social problems. Check the crime statistics and local news reports.
- Many estates have a "sinkfund" into which the residents pay. It is used for undertaking repairs to the estate. Check with the council as to what works are planned and that there is a healthy sinkfund in place.

Listed buildings

A building is "listed" when it is considered to be of special architectural or historic interest. They are called listed because all these buildings are on the National Heritage List. You can search this list by clicking on this link: https://historicengland.org.uk/listing/the-list/

It's unlikely that too many first-time buyers will be buying a listed building. Nonetheless, some will. And those that do need to be aware that if they are planning on altering the building, they will have to jump through more hoops (and are less likely to be granted permission to make these alterations). Here's what you need to know:

- 92% of listed buildings are grade II. The remaining 8% are either grade I or grade II*. It is unlikely significant alterations will be allowed to either grade I or grade II* buildings.

- If you're planning on altering or extending a listed building (or demolishing it), you have to apply for listed building consent. This is over and above planning permission.
- Each local authority will have at least one Conservation Officer who should be able to provide guidance as to what might be acceptable. The Conservation Officer should be your first port of call.

Two is better than one

If possible, I urge you to buy a property with more than one bedroom. If this is not possible, try to buy a property with room to expand. There are two reasons for this. Firstly, as a home it's more likely to remain viable for more years (and moving is expensive). Secondly, the Government offers very generous tax breaks for those renting out spare rooms. Under their rent-a-room scheme, the first £7,500 of income is tax free. That's £625 a month. Anything above this is taxed in line with your current highest tax band. Even if you don't like the thought of sharing your home, it's a great back-up should you find your finances are stretched.

Room to expand

Even if you cannot envisage overseeing lots of building work, having the option to expand your property should add value. Expanding could include a loft conversion, an extension or even a basement conversion. There is no guarantee you will get planning permission. But you are far more likely to obtain planning permission if other people on the street have done the same. For example, if other properties have converted their lofts, it's likely that planning permission will be granted for you to do the same. Precedence is very important when trying to obtain planning permission.

Note: Under the Government's Permitted Development rules, freehold houses are exempt from planning permission, provided the property is expanded within certain limits. Google "Permitted Development" for more details.

Be willing to compromise

There is probably no such thing as the perfect property, but there is such a thing as the right property. Accept you may have to compromise. It's worth being mindful of this, as otherwise you will never sign on the dotted line. A recent report by Which? identified the six most common things homebuyers compromised on. They were: price (i.e. paying more than originally intended), decor, location, room size, garden (i.e. not having any outside space or not having enough) and structural condition. The three compromises most people regretted making were: structural condition, garden and location. It's not that hard to avoid buying a property with structural issues (more on the different types of surveys later). And try not to compromise too much on the other two, especially if they are important to you. So, yes, you will have to compromise, but consider carefully which compromises you have to make.

Availability of property

Hardly a week goes by without mention of the UK's "housing crisis" - but what is this? Well it's definitely multifaceted but, in simple terms, demand is outstripping supply. The completion rate of new homes has been below the various targets set by Governments for decades. For example, in 2015, there were 170,730 new homes built, well below the consensus requirement of 250,000. In certain areas, such as London, the shortage of housing is chronic. The housing charity Shelter suggests that over a million new homes are needed, and that's just to house those in greatest need. This supply-and-demand mismatch is partly why properties are so expensive in most parts of the UK. The areas where properties are plentiful and inexpensive tend to be those with the poorest job prospects. Furthermore, most developments in the capital have been built with no intention of addressing the housing crisis. Rather, they have been built with profit maximization in mind. Take the Nine Elms Development in and around Battersea Power Station – properties in the Power Station itself start at £1.39m.

There are short-term factors too. In times of uncertainty there tend to be fewer buyers and fewer sellers. This was very notable after the vote to leave the European Union. The upshot of all these factors is this: most of the time being a buyer is tough. The properties available are often not great and there is plenty of competition for the better properties.

The decline of the Buy-To-Let investor

The Government has significantly changed the tax laws to make Buy-To-Let investing less palatable (i.e. less profitable). For example, people who own one property or more have to pay an extra 3% stamp duty on any future purchases. This additional 3% stamp duty levied on additional property purchases may have put some investors off acquiring new stock. But it's also encouraged investors to hold onto their current properties, in the knowledge that re-entering the market is now an expensive business. In addition, although market uncertainty may have discouraged some overseas property investors, when the pound falls others will be encouraged to invest. In the property world, almost nothing is linear! On balance, these changes are probably bad for domestic investors and may prove helpful for first-time buyers.

Unfortunately, there's a new kid on the block: build to rent.

Build to rent
Historically, almost all private property developments were built with one purpose: to sell the properties. Build to rent is different - these properties are being, as the name suggests, built to rent. Build to rent is attracting institutional investors, such as Legal & General, who view Generation Rent as a lucrative way to make money to bolster their pension funds. Billions has been pumped into this sector in recent years. So more properties are being built but far fewer are now for sale. This is bad news for first-time buyers.
The companies behind build to rent have suggested that it's a way to solve the current housing crisis, as has the Government, who has provided significant support, including a £1 billion build to rent fund. This is obviously nonsense. The reality is this: build to rent properties tend to be expensive to rent and are unlikely to ever be sold on the open market.

Online research
The Internet is a fantastic tool for research. For example, you can find out about new infrastructure, analyse house-price trends, identify school catchment areas and see if there's a park close by. You can also use the Internet to find properties for sale. But, if there's a bun fight to secure properties in that area, the ones featured online will be there for a reason. Perhaps they're overpriced? Perhaps they're on a busy road?

Auctions
I do not think these are suitable for first-time buyers, and this is why: properties sold via auction tend to come with "issues".

For example, some have very short leases and others have major structural defects. Auctions are also a common way for families to dispose of probate properties. The good properties that are auctioned tend to attract a lot of interest and the prices rise at the auction accordingly. And, remember, you have to have a 10% deposit ready for payment on auction day, and access to the remaining 90% within 28 days. Mind you, property auctions are very interesting events - and well worth popping along to if you want to learn more about the market.

Private sales
If you know where you'd like to live, why not leaflet viable properties in that area? Many homeowners think about selling. Maybe a little nudge is all that's needed? Set out the fact you're a first-time buyer. They will have been in the same position once.
If someone bites, the property websites are great for establishing "comparables". In other words, what's a fair price to pay? When negotiating, remember that the seller will save on estate-agent fees, which are typically between 1.5% and 4% +VAT of the selling price.

Boarded-up properties
On your property hunt, you may come across boarded-up or vacant properties. In England alone there are estimated to be over 200,000 such properties. Most of these properties will be in poor condition, but that may make them more appealing to some people. If such a property takes your fancy, you can find out who owns it by going to:
https://www.gov.uk/search-property-information-land-registry
Once you have established the ownership, write to the owners to see if they are willing to sell to you. If the answer

is yes, you may well be able to purchase this property at below the market rate.

Finding the best high-street estate agents

This is somewhat counterintuitive. Sellers want estate agents with smart offices, beautiful property photos, a welcoming receptionist, long opening hours, great Google reviews, 3D plans, elegant property descriptions, clever online marketing, helpful employees, etc. But, if you're looking for a bargain, maybe you want the opposite? Go to Foxtons for the free coffee and soft drinks. Don't buy from them. Try, instead, to find the slightly more run down estate agents. They will have less stock, but also fewer potential buyers. However, in some areas, there may be only one game in town. If that's the case, it's vital you build a good relationship with them.

Build a rapport with the estate agents

The reality is this: the best properties are snapped up before the estate agent has even drafted the details. And, given that 90% of property sales are via estate agents, it's vital you build a rapport with them. Better still, if you're able, visit them during the week, when they're less busy. Get to know their names, give them your business card (and ask for theirs), and follow up any discussions with an email. And let them know you're a great prospect.

Estate agents make their money through commission. If you can prove you're a good buyer, they're far more likely to show you the properties that have just come onto their books. Get your finances in order: a deposit in place and a mortgage agreed in principle. Also, as a first-time buyer you are chain free. (A property chain is when your purchase depends on one or more additional transactions taking place.) Many sellers will value this highly, as they know the sale is more likely to complete. Also, some sellers will favour first-time buyers over investors for reasons of principle.

Online estate agents

Online estate agents are welcome disruptors in what had become a rather staid industry. Market leaders such as Purplebricks and Yopa have been nibbling away at their high-street rivals' market share. But they are still minnows: less than 10% of all market instructions are given to online estate agents. In terms of the number of sales they represent, there are no firm figures. But I think it's safe to say 5% or less. It's worth noting that currently all the online estate agents are loss making. A series of mergers and acquisitions is likely to take place; only the fittest will survive.

Their main advantage is that they charge vendors far lower fees. Instead of charging the seller a percentage of the selling price (i.e. commission), they charge a flat fee when they list the property. The prospect of saving thousands of pounds in commission has encouraged some sellers to jump ship. But how does this affect first-time buyers? Although their market share is small, the online estate agents cannot be ignored. The lower fees mean the seller may be willing to sell for slightly less too. Also, most people selling online arrange their own viewings. This gives you the chance to get to know the seller.

On the flipside, as online estate agents earn their money once the property is listed, they may be less motivated to push the sale through to completion. (Completion is when traditional estate agents get paid by the seller.)

Online estate agents advertise their properties on their own website and on various property portals such as Rightmove and Zoopla. They also use far-from-online "For Sale" boards.

Moreover, they are perfectly poised to take advantage of new technologies, such as virtual property tours.

Property portals and apps

Most properties for sale in the UK can be found on either Zoopla or Rightmove. These websites work with online and traditional high-street estate agents - both of whom pay to have the properties on their books featured on these websites. At time of writing, Rightmove had slightly over a million properties for sale, whereas Zoopla had slightly below a million. Both have tens of millions of visits per month. These websites are too big to ignore. But don't discount OnTheMarket. OnTheMarket was set up by a consortium of UK estate agents as a rival to Zoopla and Rightmove. Currently the OnTheMarket website gets far fewer monthly visits, but they do advertise properties 24 hours before they are listed on the main property portals. If you're fleet of foot, that 24-hour head start could prove very useful.

The property portals allow you to search properties in various ways - definitely check out "map view" and "recently added". As you would expect, the three property portals described above have apps. They all have pros and cons. Zoopla's property search and property price history tools are excellent. You can also find properties by travel time from, for example, your workplace.

Buying agents/property finders

Buying agents are companies or individuals that will find a property on your behalf. They were popularised by television programmes such as Location Location Location. And, while they still predominantly operate at the top end of the property market, there is now a buying agent to suit almost all pursestrings.

Buying agents were set up remove the legwork of hunting for a property. Typically, they will meet with prospective buyers to ascertain their wants, needs and limiting factors. Some will ask for a written brief too. The buying agent will then create a shortlist of properties. It's then up to you: you can reject them all or you can view as many as you like. Traditionally, buying agents charge an up-front fee. In addition, should you purchase one of the properties they have sourced, you would pay them a percentage of the purchase price, in the region of 2%. However, times are changing. The top-end agents still charge an up-front fee, but recently buying agents have emerged who only charge upon completion. Within this group is a subset who charge flat-rate fees.

There are also agents who only charge a percentage of the amount they save the buyer – 15% seems to be the industry norm. So, if they negotiated a £40,000 discount, you would pay them £6,000.

Buying agents are only as good as their industry relationships. The top-end agents will get much of their business via word of mouth. It's reckoned that 20% of million-pound-plus properties are not sold on the open market – instead vendors approach buying agents directly. Buying agents will also have contacts with estate agents, surveyors and developers. They get to see the properties first, which means you do too. They also know the market so they can ensure you don't overpay. In fact, by removing the competition you may find they save you far more money than they cost. The end result (in theory) is a better property for less money, and with far less hassle.

In addition, you're the client. Estate agents, ultimately, work for sellers – that's who pays their fees. Buying agents work for buyers. As such, they are far more likely to listen to your concerns and feedback. Estate agents often blanket email properties to people on their books, with no thought of their requirements. Buying agents separate wheat from chaff.

Are buying agents suitable for first-time buyers?

If you can find a buying agent that doesn't charge an up-front fee, this feels like a no-risk option. However, some areas are less well serviced by buying agents. And some buying agents only deal with the top end of the market. A quick Google search will help you find out whether there's a viable buying agent operating in your search area.

Viewing properties

You've narrowed down your search, arranged a mortgage in principle and befriended estate agents. Now is the fun part: property viewings. There are basically two types of viewings: sole or group. The latter could involve up to a dozen prospective buyers viewing the same property at the same time. If possible, avoid these. It's much harder to ask questions and inspect the property properly.

Slow down

Buying a property, for most people, is the biggest financial decision of their lives. Yet, according to various reports, most people spend less than 25 minutes viewing their prospective home. Given the price of the average UK property, this is, undoubtedly, a very expensive per-minute decision. So, take your time: carefully inspect the property and the location. And take lots of photos and ask lots of questions. Do not feel pressured by the estate agent - it's your money on the line, not theirs. If they try to rush you, ignore them! If you leave with unanswered questions, make a note of them and send a follow-up email to the estate agent.

Property-viewing checklist:
The roof. If you're able, arrive early and spend some time carefully inspecting the roof. Stand back from the property and look at the roof. If the ridgeline isn't horizontal, sagging has occurred. There are many reasons this may have happened. Often it's because the original timbers have been clad with heavy concrete roof tiles without having been reinforced. A sagging roof will need to be replaced in due course and the timbers may need to be reinforced. (If you are planning on undertaking a loft conversion, this could be an astute purchase as you can negotiate on price, knowing you will replace the roof anyway.) Other things to look out for include missing slates, leaking/blocked gutters and leaning chimneys. Only the most obvious things will be visible without a closer inspection. But, at this stage, this is fine.
The walls. Larger cracks may have been caused by subsidence. Ask the owner whether the property has been underpinned and what guarantees are in place. Smaller cracks are usually the result of historic movement and should be of little concern. Bowing or bulging external walls are usually caused by the original walls being insufficiently thick or misaligned floor joists/beams bearing down incorrectly. To rectify significant cracks or bulging could be expensive. If they are obvious, get a full structural survey. (More on surveys later.) Look for signs of damp too. Dark staining is the giveaway sign. If you do see these, is there an obvious cause? Perhaps there's a leaking overflow pipe or an issue with the guttering.
You should also inspect the pointing between the bricks. If it crumbles when you scrape it with your fingernail, that's not a

---

good sign. Poor pointing will allow water to seep into the walls.

The boiler. How old is it? Is it serviced annually? If the boiler is more than eight years old it will need to be replaced in the next few years. If it has not been regularly serviced, it might be dangerous.

Damp. There are three main types of damp: rising damp, condensation and penetrating damp. Rising damp is caused by groundwater rising, via capillary action, up the walls or through the floor of properties. Rising damp is very common in properties built before 1875, but is not uncommon in newer properties. After 1875, most properties were constructed with damp-proof courses built into the walls and damp-proof membranes installed under the floors. Here's how you spot rising damp: look for black spots, peeling wallpaper, rotting skirting boards, tide marks on the walls or a damp smell. In kitchens lino is often installed over damp floors to hide rising damp. The next type of damp is condensation. This is caused by the difference in air temperature between the inside and the outside. As such, it's often far more of a problem in the winter. Condensation used to be very uncommon in older properties as they were designed to breathe. Then people started removing fireplaces, blocking up air bricks and installing double glazing without vents - all of these things have led to more condensation in older properties. Here's how you spot condensation: misted up windows, water droplets on walls, dark mould on window frames or a damp smell. Finally there's penetrating damp. Penetrating damp is caused by water penetration external walls. This affects older properties far more, in particular stone structures and end-of-terrace properties. It may also affect properties with cracks in the walls and poor pointing.

Here's how you spot penetrating damp: damp patches on the internal walls, which will be worse after heavy rain.

The ceilings. Check they are level and free from damp patches. Even minor leaks in the pipework will cause staining.

Dry rot. This is caused by a fungus and, if there is dampness in the property, the fungal spores can germinate on the wood. It then sends out hyphae (grey/white strands of fungal growth) in search of more wood to feed off. These strands can cause catastrophic damage to a property. Any wall badly affected by dry rot will crumble and have to be rebuilt. The tell-tale signs are a mushroom-like smell, cracking timber, spore dust and grey strands. Dry rot is pretty rare. Plus, any half-decent surveyor should spot it if you don't.

Electrics. Rewiring a property is expensive and messy - countless floorboards will have to be pulled up and holes will have to be cut into the brickwork for sockets, etc. Are there enough power sockets in each room? Are they free from stains and cracks? Look at the fuse box too. Does it look new?

Parking space/cost of parking. Does the property have an allocated parking space? If not, is it possible to buy one? If there's on-street parking, do you need a permit to park there? If so, how much does it cost? Beware, some new build properties in city centres come without the right to on-street parking. In other words, if you apply for a parking permit your application will be rejected.

Bathrooms. Bathrooms are expensive to update. Can you live with the bathrooms the way they are? Are the taps free from limescale? Is the bathroom suite free from chips/stains? Is the room free of damp marks? Is the mastic (sealant) and grout still white?

Water pressure. There's nothing more disappointing than a shower that dribbles. Check the hot and cold taps.

Windows. Check the windows open and close properly. But ask first - some people won't like you doing this. Windows that don't open might have been painted shut or may be warped. Are the windows double-glazed? If so, do they have trickle vents (small vents at the top or the bottom that help prevent damp). Are the window frames wood, PVC or aluminium? If they are wooden, is the wood in a good state of repair and have they been freshly painted? If they are PVC is the plastic stained? Aluminium windows tend to be quite ugly and could put off future buyers.

What direction does the garden/balcony face? In the UK, most property experts advocate buying a home with a south-facing garden. Gardens that face south receive the most light; gardens that face north receive the least light and can be damp; gardens that face east receive light in the morning; gardens that face west receive light in the late afternoon and evening. But, of course, it all depends on your preferences. Larks may favour an east-facing garden; night owls may favour a west-facing garden. Top tip: download a compass app for your smartphone.

Woodchip wallpaper. If the walls and or ceilings are lined with woodchip wallpaper, this is usually a bad sign. Woodchip is most commonly used to disguise crumbling plaster. If you try to remove it you'll probably find the plaster crumbles off too. Replastering is expensive and messy.

Woodworm. If you're able to inspect the floorboards, look for woodworm holes. Active woodworm holes will often have fine powdery dust near them. Also, some holes will look newer than others. Old inactive woodworm holes should not be a concern - the woodworm has most likely been eradicated. If you're unsure if they're active, ask if there are any guarantees in place. All reputable woodworm-eradication specialists will supply these.

Drains. If you're feeling brave, lift the drain covers and check they are free from blockages and tree roots.

Attic. If there's an attic, and you're able to look up there, check for insulation between the ceiling joists and that there's felt between the roof joists and roof tiles. If there's no roof felt, the roof is almost certainly more than 50 years old and may need to be replaced.

Radiators. Are they free from rust? Check the bottoms and where they're joined to the pipework.

Guarantees. Ask if there are any guarantees in place for work previously undertaken. For example, the seller may have installed a new roof.

Storage. One of the most common problems with newer properties is the lack of storage. Where will you store your bike, your suitcases, your printer, your paperwork, your bedding, etc.?

Bins. Is there room for the various bins you need? Some councils require multiple bins for rubbish, recycling, food waste, etc. Is there space for all of these?

Communal areas. If there are communal areas, spend more time inspecting these than would seem natural. They can tell you a lot about the area, the management company and your neighbours. Some things to check:

- Are they free from litter?
- Are the carpets in good order?
- Does the intercom system work?
- Have the walls been painted recently?
- Are the main entrances locked? Do they look secure?
- Are the communal gardens well maintained?

- Is there a noticeboard? If so, check it has up-to-date notices and useful information and contact numbers.

Japanese Knotweed. Japanese Knotweed was introduced into the UK by Victorian engineers to hide/stabilise unsightly railway embankments. The problem is this: Japanese Knotweed is a pernicious plant that can grow through tarmac, destroy drains, and can grow under and through foundations. Plus, it can grow as fast as 10cm a day, with the roots growing up to three metres deep. Google: "Japanese Knotweed" so you know what it looks like and be especially careful if you are buying near a railway line. You can find crowd-sourced data on known Japanese Knotweed locations by clicking this link:
http://www.planttracker.org.uk/map/knotweed

Leylandii. Leylandii is a common form of evergreen hedge. Its main advantages are that it's fast growing and provides excellent privacy. But that's also its main downfall. If left unpruned, the green species of Leylandii can grow up to 25m high. Leylandii hedges are one of the most common causes of neighbour disputes.

Property-viewing checklist (desk research)

Price per square foot. In many markets across the world, the price per square foot (or per square metre) is one of the first things people look at. For some unknown reason, this is far less common in the UK. If the estate agent doesn't provide this information, simply divide the price by the number of square feet. This is a great way to compare the prices of similar properties. Cluttered properties are often overlooked because they feel smaller. The opposite is true of sparsely furnished show homes - people overpay because they feel spacious. Calculating the price per square foot takes the emotion out of your decision-making process.

Energy Performance Certificate (EPC). All properties on the market need to have an up-to-date EPC, which shows you how energy efficient the property currently is and how efficient it has the potential to become. An EPC gives a property an energy efficiency rating from A (most efficient) to G (least efficient). As EPCs are valid for 10 years, sometimes the information will be out of date. For example, the seller may have installed double glazing since the EPC was issued. EPCs also include recommendations about how to reduce energy use. The less energy efficient a property is, the more it will cost to run. There are some low-cost ways to improve energy efficiency (such as insulating attics). Others, such as replacing an old boiler, are far more expensive.

Council tax. The amount of council tax you pay can vary widely, depending on the local authority and the type/size of property. Ask the estate agent how much the current owner is paying. If they fail to provide this information, you can find out the answer here: https://www.gov.uk/council-tax-bands

Planning permission. If the property has obviously been altered - for example, there's now a bedroom in the loft space - have the relevant permissions been obtained? If the seller does not have the relevant paperwork, you can check on the local authority's website.

Building control. In addition to planning permission, all significant building work should have been signed off by building control. Again, if the seller does not have the relevant paperwork, you can check on the local authority's website.

Floorplans. These are useful in determining how viable each room is and whether there's the potential to extend. For example, is there room for a double bed in all of the bedrooms?

Street-viewing checklist:

It's not enough to decide on the area - being one street in the wrong direction can make a significant difference.

Noise. The causes of noise, especially in cities, are countless. Cars, aeroplanes, trains, nightspots, sirens, neighbours, etc. If you're viewing the property on a cold day, open the windows and listen. Also, consider the different times of day. Some streets are very quiet during the day, but are noisy when the lights go down. The opposite is also true. There are oddities too: if there are road humps or bus stops too close, expect the sound of braking vehicles.

Street lighting. Well-lit streets are great in terms of safety, but not so good if there's a light that shines into your bedroom. Blackout blinds are an easy fix for the latter.

Litter/bins. Is the street free from litter? If there are communal bins will they affect you in a negative way? For example, the smell and the noise of them being emptied early one morning each week.

Front gardens/doors. If the nearby properties are in a good state of repair, it's a good sign that this is a good street. It also indicates that most of the properties are owner-occupied. This is important as, it could be argued, that tenants have a less vested interest in that community and maintaining the property.

Freehold or Leasehold

In simple terms, if you buy a freehold property, you own the building and the land upon which the building sits. Leasehold means that you "own" the property for a set period of time, but not the land on which the property sits.

How many properties are leasehold?

The Department for Communities and Local Government (DCLG) estimates that there are 4.2 million leasehold properties in England alone. A further 200,000 properties in Wales are estimated to be leasehold too. It's also estimated that 43% of new-build properties are now sold as leasehold. In London, that rises to 90%. If you are planning on buying a property in Scotland or Northern Ireland, you have permission to gloat. Legislation passed by the Scottish parliament has effectively brought leasehold to an end in Scotland. The Scottish parliament should be congratulated for this. Leaseholders in Northern Ireland are better off too, as they have the right to buy their freehold for about ten times the ground rent. (In England and Wales the cost of buying the freehold will be affected by a number of factors, the main ones being the length of time left on each lease and the ground-rent charges. Typically it will cost three to four times as much compared to owners in Northern Ireland. More on this later.)

Leasehold issues

Recent research concluded that over 90% of owners of leasehold properties regretted buying a leasehold property. Moreover, almost 60% didn't know the difference between a freehold property and a leasehold property when they signed on the dotted line. So, what is the difference?

- As mentioned above, if you buy a freehold property you own the building and the land upon which the building has been built. Almost all houses are freehold. Leasehold means that you "own" the property for a set period of time, but not the land on which the property sits.

- All leasehold properties have a lease, which, among other things, details the length of time you can occupy and use the property. This will range from one year to 999 years.
- Once a lease drops below 80 years the value of the property begins to fall and this drop in value accelerates rapidly once the lease drops to less than 60 years. The main reason is the difficulty of obtaining a mortgage for such properties. Lenders invariably stipulate a minimum unexpired lease term. For example, there may need to be 70 years left on the lease to satisfy your lender's lending criteria. Some lenders will have a lower limit. However, the choice of lenders will be limited if you have a short lease, which means you won't get access to the best rates. Worse still, some leases are so short that the property becomes "unmortgageable" – therefore these properties can only be sold to cash buyers.

Ground rent and service charges

The main additional costs leaseholders have to pay are ground rent and service charges. Both are paid to the Freeholder. Some ground rents are "peppercorn" (i.e. a token amount, say £1 a year); others can run to thousands of pounds a year. Each lease is unique and the reasons for the various differences are wide and disparate. Even if your ground rent is minimal, make sure you pay this to ensure you're not in breach of the lease.

Service charges also have to be paid to the Freeholder. These include such things as maintaining communal gardens, electricity bills for communal areas, repair and maintenance of exterior walls, windows and roofs. You will also need to pay your share of the buildings insurance. The freeholder will invoice you these costs.

Recent research found that 53% of homeowners in London have regrets about buying their property due to service-charge costs. According to the Homeowners Alliance's research, 26% of leaseholders complained about the high cost of works and management fees, 22% objected to unfair service charges, and a further 23% had issues with the lack of control over which major works were undertaken.

ARMA (the Association of Residential Managing Agents) estimates the average service charge bill in London at around £1,800 to £2,000 a year. That's a lot of money! It has also been reported that some homeowners have found it impossible to sell due to unattractive high service charges. Make sure you are aware of the service charges and factor these into your budget calculations. There are ways to reduce your service charges, but it is far from straightforward. (See "Buying a property with high service charges".)

Leasehold covenants

Leasehold covenants are included in most leases. Most are reasonable and are put in place to prevent anti-social behaviour. Some, however, will affect what you can do to your property and how you use your property. Here are a list of common things that are banned due to leasehold covenants:

- Using your home as a holiday let. In the AirBnB era, this is far from ideal.
- Sub-letting your property. In other words, you will be unable to rent out your property in the future. Also, technically, you may not be able to rent your spare room to a tenant. (Although most freeholders will turn a blind eye to this.)

- Running a business from your property. Again, this feels very dated. In recent years there's been a huge rise in people working from home and self-employment.
- Keeping pets. This is very common and usually even includes birds.
- Having wooden or laminate flooring.
- Making too much noise. This includes DIY, playing music, watching TV too loudly or hosting parties during antisocial hours.
- If there's a communal forecourt, the number and type of vehicles you're allowed to park there may be restricted. For example, commercial vehicles, such as vans, may be banned.

These are just some examples. Leasehold covenants vary from lease to lease and you need to read the lease carefully to see what's included.

Restrictive covenants

These can affect both leasehold and freehold properties. Restrictive covenants are legally-binding conditions that are written into a property's deeds or contract by a seller. Most properties have no restrictive covenants. But, if they do exist, make sure you understand them. Here are some common examples:
- Clauses that prevent owners running a business from their property.
- Clauses that prevent owners making significant alterations to their property. This could include extending the property.

Understanding the lease

The first thing to know is that most property documentation is in the public domain. If you are interested in a property, most leases are available to download: https://www.gov.uk/search-property-information-land-registry

Your solicitor will look at the lease too, but there are plenty of cases where poor conveyancing has taken place and lease issues have been missed, the most significant of which often involve rising ground rent. This is a real-life example: The ground rent payable was £500 a year. But within the lease was provision for this to be doubled every ten years. That doesn't sound too onerous until you play things forward. In 60 years the ground rent would be £32,000 and after 70 it's £64,000 etc. After 100 years the property would probably be worthless to all bar one person: the freeholder. This would also affect your right to extend the lease or buy the freehold. More on that later.

So, while it isn't incumbent on you to understand every word of the lease, you should read it and ask lots of questions.

Rogue freeholders

Most freeholders are reasonable. However, there are unscrupulous freeholders too. Freeholds can be bought and sold on the open market. This has led to the situation whereby big companies have acquired thousands of individual freeholds. And, more often than not, the freeholders have no personal relationship with the leaseholders.

In a recent case, a freeholder tried to charge the two leaseholders £40,000 to replace their roof. This job should have cost in the region of £10,000. After much toing and froing and threatening emails the freeholder eventually backed down and agreed that the leaseholders could appoint their own roofers. In effect, the freeholder was overcharging with a view to then getting a "kick back" from the builders. This is not as uncommon as you would think. Other freeholders have been accused of hiking service charges to unacceptably high levels. Also, if you're a leaseholder and want to reconfigure, enhance or expand your property, you need to apply for a licence for alterations. This can take some time and you will need to pay a fee.

Buying a property with a short lease
Properties with short leases definitely sell at a discounted price. This is especially the case when the lease has dropped below 80 years, as some lenders will not offer mortgages on such properties. That being said, sometimes it's a very good way to snap up a bargain. There are two ways to add value to this kind of property: extending the lease or buying the freehold.

Extending a lease
Leaseholders can ask the freeholder to extend their lease at any time. And you have the right to extend your lease once you've owned your property for two years. (There are some exceptions, but these are few and far between.) The cost of extending the lease depends on the following factors:
- The length of the current lease.
- The length of the proposed lease extension.
- The current and *future* ground rent. Note: some leases have a provision for ground-rent increases. You should probably avoid buying any such property, unless these increases are minimal. (If, as mentioned before, the ground rent was due to double every ten years, the cost of extending the lease could be

prohibitively high, thus making the property virtually valueless.)

- The current value of the property.
- The value of the property after lease extension.
- The yield rate (which, post Cadogan v Sportelli (2006), is normally set at 5%). This is used to calculate the "term" (i.e. the loss of future ground rent). Valuers will use this figure and the length of the current lease to ascertain the value of the term. If the current and future ground rent is low, the term amount will also be low.
- You will also need to pay your and the freeholder's legal fees.
- If the cost of extending the lease is over £125,000 (which is very rare) you would also be liable to pay stamp duty.

This nifty tool provides a lease-extension costs "general estimate": https://www.lease-advice.org/calculator/

In effect, the price of the lease extension has been designed to compensate the freeholder for:

- The loss of ground rent (should you negotiate a lower ground rent).
- Reduced "reversion" value of the property. (If a lease drops to 0 years, the freeholder assumes ownership of the property. This is known as "reversion". Therefore the freeholder effectively suffers a loss due to the additional wait for this reversion.)

This area of law is pretty complex. Make sure you employ a specialist lease-extension solicitor. They will be able to calculate the cost of extending the lease and negotiate with the freeholder on your behalf. Ideally, the freeholder will agree with your solicitor's valuation. But, if not, you may need to take the case to the Leasehold Valuation Tribunal.

Leases below 80 years
If the lease is less than 80 years, the freeholder is also entitled to a "Marriage Value". In simple terms, this is 50% of the uplift in the property value post lease extension. So, for example, if a property was worth £300,000 before the lease extension and £315,000 after the lease extension, the freeholder would be entitled to an additional £7,500.

Top tip: If you are extending a lease and the freeholder suggests increasing the ground rent in a manner that allows for substantial future increases, do not agree to this. It could render your property valueless.

Should a first-time buyer buy a property with a short lease?
Extending a lease is a time-consuming, annoying process that's riddled with nuances. This is why so many people take the head-in-the-sand approach (which is why there are lots of properties for sale with short leases). I would not recommend buying any property with a lease of less than 83 years (as that gives you time to extend the lease once you've lived there for two years without paying the "Marriage Value"). For further, more detailed information, go to the Lease Advice website (which is excellent): https://www.lease-advice.org/

Buying a freehold
As an alternative (and some would say a better alternative) to extending the lease, you may be able to buy a share of the freehold. In simple terms, in most cases, you need 50% (or

more) of the leaseholders on board to purchase a share of freehold. So, if you bought a leasehold property in a block of six flats, if three leaseholders (or more) agreed to buy the freehold, you should be able to do this. It's worth noting that the more leaseholders involved the more complex the freehold purchase becomes. If you buy the freehold, you are responsible for maintaining, repairing and insuring the property - you may have to set up a company to manage the building or find a managing agent who can do this on your behalf. However, the benefits are numerous:

- No more ground rent.
- Reduced service charges.
- The opportunity to extend your lease for peanuts.
- The opportunity to remove leasehold covenants.
- The opportunity to alter your property without freeholder consent.
- You will no longer be beholden to the freeholder.

Your lease will still run alongside the freehold but, collectively, you can amend your leases in any way that's beneficial to all parties. For example, you could agree to increase all your leases to 999 years. For this you would only pay legal costs.

To buy the freehold you will need to get a competent solicitor to serve a Section 13 Notice on the freeholder. Before you do this, you will need to get the freehold valued. As with extending a lease, the cost of buying the freehold is affected by a number of factors, the main ones being the length of time left on each lease, the current and future ground rent charges, and the development potential of the property. Ideally, the current lease will be long and the ground rent will be low. Your solicitor will be able to appoint a specialist to value the freehold.

———

Most freeholders willingly agree to sell the freehold, as the valuation is formulaic. As such, why contest it? If they do, they are highly unlikely to receive a higher compensation. But, freeholders are humans and humans are irrational. This means, in some cases, the purchase price will be contested and you may have to go to a tribunal. You are liable for all the freeholder's legal costs, including any tribunal costs.

Buying a property with high service charges
As mentioned above, one way to reduce your service charges is to buy the freehold. But, for some leaseholders, this may not be an option. The next best alternative is obtaining the "Right to Manage" (RTM). This means that the leaseholders manage all the maintenance of the building and they notify the freeholder when work is being carried out. The Right to Manage lets some leasehold property owners take over management of the building - even without the agreement of the landlord.
These are the main criteria that have to be met:
- The building must be made up of flats (houses don't qualify).
- At least two-thirds of the flats in the building must be leasehold - with leases that were for more than 21 years when they were granted.
- At least 75% of the building must be residential. For example, if there's a shop in the building, it can't take up more than 25% of the total floor area.

Leaseholders must set up an RTM company. To form a Right to Manage company, agreement is required from a minimum of 50% of apartment owners in the building. The RTM company can manage the building directly, or pay a managing agent to do this. The RTM company must pay for

any costs incurred during the management transfer process -
even if it doesn't end up managing the building.

Members of the RTM company have the right to vote on
decisions. Typically, each leaseholder gets one vote.
Freeholders will get one vote too (or more if they have a
leasehold interest in some of the properties).

The benefits of Right to Manage:

- Greater transparency over how costs are incurred.
- Control over which suppliers/contractors are used.
- Reduced service charges.
- You're no longer at the mercy of unprincipled
  freeholders.

The downsides of Right to Manage:

- There is definitely a time cost. The RTM company
  will be responsible for such things as collecting and
  managing the service charge, upkeep of communal
  areas (such as communal hallways and stairs),
  upkeep of the structure of the building (such as the
  roof), arranging buildings insurance and dealing with
  complaints about the building from other
  leaseholders.
- Disagreements between leaseholders. Right to
  Manage is definitely more democratic, but autocratic
  states do tend to get things done quicker!

Buying a wreck

Sometimes the only way you will be able to afford a property
in your desired area is to buy a run-down property. This
option won't be suitable for all first-time buyers, but it is a
good way to get onto the property ladder and to add value to
the property. After all, this is how property developers make
their livelihood. Some things to consider:

- In some areas, the competition for run-down properties will be fierce. You will be up against seasoned property developers, some of whom will be cash buyers. This means you may have to convince the seller (and the estate agent) that you are a viable buyer.
- Lenders will consider some run-down properties unmortgageable. As such, only cash buyers will be considered.
- Do you have contacts in the building trade? If so, ask them to estimate how much the work will cost. And, maybe, ask them to do the work if you take ownership. If you don't have any such contacts, there are lots of excellent websites that will put you in touch with tradespeople. For example, https://www.fmb.org.uk/find-a-builder/; https://www.checkatrade.com/ and https://www.ratedpeople.com
- Some lenders will want to see plans and estimates of proposed works.
- You should be willing to learn how to undertake certain jobs yourself (and willing to sacrifice your weekends to do these jobs). The information age has made acquiring knowledge much easier - there are YouTube videos showing you how to do every DIY job imaginable.
- Be prepared for setbacks. Most old properties have hidden secrets, such as rotting joists under the floorboards or crumbling plaster under the woodchip wallpaper.

By the way, this is a fun website: www.wreckoftheweek.co.uk

Making an offer

If the property is being sold through an estate agent you need to make your offer to the estate agent. This can be done verbally or in writing. I urge you to do both (i.e. call and then follow up with an email). This offer isn't legally binding. Indeed, it's assumed that this offer is 'subject to contract'. In other words, further negotiation can take place. (In Scotland, there's a different process - more on that later.)

But, before you make an offer, try to find out as much as possible about the seller's position and how much competition there is from other potential buyers.

How long has the property been on the market? If the property has been on the market for more than three months, the likelihood is that there has been little interest. This puts you in a strong position.

Is the seller in a property chain? Remember, a property chain is when your purchase depends on one or more additional transactions taking place. For example, does the seller need to buy another property before they can sell? The more complicated the chain, the longer you may have to wait to get the property. It also increases the chances of the sale not completing. On the plus side, first-time buyers are always welcome additions to property chains, as they are "chain free" (i.e. first-time buyers don't have a property to sell).

How many viewings have taken place? Ask the estate agent if there has been much interest. If they are cagey with their answer, that usually means "not many". If, after all, there have been loads of viewings, you'll be the first to know.

Is the seller on the run? There are a few telltale signs that a seller is desperate to sell. Firstly, if you see the property for sale with more than one estate agent. Secondly, if the estate agent has reduced the price. If this is the case, you may find yourself in a strong negotiating position. Also, knowing their personal circumstances can help. It's an unpleasant truth that things such as divorce, bankruptcy, death and the threat of being repossessed can often lead to people being desperate to sell.

Has a sale fallen through? Sometimes you'll find a seller who has been let down by a buyer. This may have caused a complicated property chain to collapse. Such sellers may be desperate to find a first-time buyer who can move fast. If that's you, negotiate hard on the price.

The state of the market. I urge you to start reading the business news and every property article you chance upon. That aside, it's quite easy to ascertain the state of the market in your area by how the estate agents act. In a rising market, estate agents can be nonchalant to the point of rudeness - they won't return your calls and don't reply to emails, etc. In a flat market, estate agents morph into sycophants. In a rising market, you will need to act fast and sometimes pay a little over the odds. In a flat market, negotiate hard.

Everyone (and every seller) has their price

Once you know these things you can make an informed offer. But, before you settle on your offer price, talk to the estate agent and try to ascertain the trigger price. Most sellers will have a figure in their head below which they will be reluctant to sell. And this figure will almost certainly be below the asking price. You can now make an offer. If you have discovered the seller is desperate to sell and the market is flat, do not be afraid to offer well below the asking price. The seller can only say, no. And, if they do say no, ask them how much they will accept. Do not increase your offer until they have demonstrated a willingness to negotiate. Get them to make a counter offer. Once they have moved down, you could suggest splitting the difference. This shifts the price downwards again. If you still think the price is too high, ask them to include certain items in the sale. For example, the fridge and the washing machine. As a first-time buyer, the cost of furnishing a property could be considerable. This is one way to reduce that burden.

Of course, some properties will have garnered a lot of interest. In this case, it's crucial you don't get sucked into a bidding war. Write down the highest price you are willing to pay and stick to this.

Standing out from the crowd

If the vendor has received multiple offers, you need to tread carefully. It's easy to be sucked into a bidding war and paying well over the odds. Instead, carefully explain why they should accept your offer over the others. Here are some things you could include in your argument:

- Reiterate your market position: You're a chain-free first-time buyer.
- If you're coming to the end of your tenancy, try to negotiate a rolling monthly contract. This will increase your ability to align your timings with the seller's. Moreover, it should help you avoid the nightmare scenario of having to pay rent and a mortgage for a period of time.
- Your mortgage has already been agreed in principle.
- Promise you will instruct your lender to obtain a property valuation/undertake a survey the day your offer is accepted.
- You have a solicitor lined up (more on finding the best conveyancing solicitors later).

- Your willingness to compromise. This is particularly important in terms of timing. Say you will fit around the seller's timings. Sellers invariably welcome this as they will probably be dealing with at least one sale and one purchase.

Also:

- Be professional. Estates agents are invariably awash with potential buyers. Make sure you return calls and reply to emails – written communication is vital, even if you're just reiterating earlier conversations. And don't forget to say "please" and "thank you"!
- If you're fortunate enough to meet the vendor – and you should push for this - sell your dream. Properties aren't just bricks and mortar, they are people's homes and come with all the associated memories. That makes people sentimental – they want to like the person who's going to live there when they move out. Reassure them that you will take care of the property. And, if you're about to get married, have children or, of course, buy your first property (or anything else that could resonate) share your hopes and dreams. As I mentioned before, many sellers would prefer to sell to someone who wants to make the property a home. If you're neck-and-neck with an investor, this could swing things in your favour.

Sealed bids

Some sellers will require all prospective buyers to submit sealed bids. A sealed-bid sale requires all bidders (prospective buyers) to simultaneously submit sealed bids to the estate agent so that no bidder knows how much the other prospective buyers have offered. The highest bidder will usually be declared the winner.

If you find yourself in this situation, try not to second-guess what your competition are going to bid. Rather, bid what you are willing to pay. But, if that's a round figure, maybe add £150 (as someone else might think the same as you, and it's common for people to add £100 to their bid).

Your offer is accepted - do not celebrate yet!

You've agreed the price. You've shaken hands with the seller. You've started mentally visualising living in your dream home. What could go wrong? Quite a lot actually: research shows that between 25% and 30% of accepted offers never reach exchange.

Part 4 - From offer to completion

What's next?

Once your offer has been accepted, you need to do the following things:

- Make sure the estate agent stops advertising the property. Ask for the details to be removed from their window, their website and the property-portal websites. (In fact, you can make this a condition of your offer.) A few days later, check the estate agent has done what you requested.
- Inform your solicitor, in writing, of the accepted offer. Copy the estate agent into this email. (More on finding a solicitor later.) You should ask for the seller's solicitor's contact details too.
- Review your lending options. You may have a mortgage in principle approved, but the market may have moved in your favour. New mortgage products are released every week. Talk to your mortgage advisor - are there now better options available?
- Book a survey. Your lender will appoint an independent surveyor for this task. So tell your mortgage advisor that your offer has been accepted and ask them to ask your lender to book the survey. (More on choosing the right survey for you later.)

What could go wrong now?

The common reasons accepted offers don't reach exchange include:

- The buyer being unable to secure a mortgage. Hopefully, with a mortgage in principle in place this won't happen to you.

- Issues with the survey. (More on this later.)
- The chain collapses. The more interlinking properties in the chain, the greater the chance of this happening.
- Being gazumped. This is when the buyer has accepted one offer only to then accept another higher offer from another buyer. As mentioned above, getting the property taken off the market will definitely reduce the chances of this happening. You may also be able to agree a lock-in agreement with the seller. A lock-in agreement is legally binding and commits the seller to avoiding dealing with other parties during a fixed period of time. Normally both parties would pay a deposit that they risk losing if they break this agreement (unless there is good reason to do so - for example, the survey results unearth major problems with the property). I can't help but think that lock-in agreements are a bit over the top. They are very uncommon too.
- Gazundering. This is when the buyer lowers their offer from the accepted offer price. This is acceptable if there's good reason (again, such as poor survey results). But, do this at your peril. The seller could drop you as a buyer and estate agents could start to dislike you.
- The seller changes their mind. They are not legally obliged to sell to you until you have exchanged contracts. Moving swiftly to this point is, therefore, very desirable.
- Unscrupulous seller. Some sellers will try to change the price before exchange, change the timescales unreasonably, or secretly keep the property on the

market. If you detect any of these things happening, I
urge you to walk away from the deal.

You cannot control all of these, but you can increase your
chance of success. Keep on top of your solicitor, phone the
estate agent every week, keep in constant contact with your
mortgage advisor. As the buyer, you'll need to crack the
whip.

Joint ownership

As mentioned before, it is possible for ownership of a
property to be split between up to four people - although, in
practice, two is the most common by far. If you're buying a
property with a partner or friend, there are two types of joint
ownership:

Joint tenancy. This is the most common type of ownership
for married couples or those in committed relationships. As
joint tenants, you must act as a single owner. If one of the
owners dies, their share of the property automatically goes to
the surviving owner/owners. So, in your will, you cannot
leave your share of the property to someone else. In
addition, if you want to sell the property, all parties must
agree to this.

Tenancy in common. This is the most common type of
ownership for friends or relatives who are buying together. In
this case, each party owns a share of the property. Typically
this means 50% each. But this can be split any way you
choose. You can leave your share of the property to anyone
you choose to name in your will. Technically each owner
could also have their own mortgage; in reality this never
happens. As with joint tenancy, if you want to sell the
property, all parties must agree to this.

Cohabitation agreement

The fastest growing type of homeownership is cohabitation. This includes everyone buying with someone else, when the individuals are not married or not in a civil partnership. Owners who cohabit have fewer legal rights compared to those who are married or those who are in a civil partnership. As such, getting a cohabitation agreement drafted is essential.

A cohabitation agreement allows you to document how you will split your property, if your relationship breaks down. It can also include the contents, personal belongings, debts, savings and other assets. If you have children you can detail how they will be supported over and above any current legal requirements. It can also include how you plan to pay the mortgage or household bills.

Google: "cohabitation agreement" to find legal advice. There are free templates you can use, but getting proper advice is always better. Expect to pay £500 +VAT for a cohabitation agreement.

Conveyancing

Conveyancing is the transfer of a legal title of a property from one person to another. In the UK it is almost exclusively undertaken by conveyancing solicitors. Finding a good conveyancing solicitor can be the difference between successfully securing the property and losing it. On average, the conveyancing process takes between 10 to 12 weeks, although it often takes longer, especially if there's a chain involved. As part of the process, your solicitor will undertake property searches. These include the following:

Local authority searches. These are the main things included in a local authority search:

- Is it a listed building?

- Is the property located in a conservation area?
- Is there a tree-protection order in place? If so, you will not be able to cut down the affected trees.
- Has the property been deemed in need of an improvement or renovation grant?
- Is the property located in a smoke-control zone? If so, you will be restricted as to what you can burn in an open fire or woodburner.
- Are there any plans for new roads or rail schemes that could affect the property?
- Are there any planning decisions that could affect the property?
- Is the property subject to a compulsory purchase order?
- Does the property stand on contaminated land?

Environmental searches. These include, for example, flood risks (from coastal, river or surface water flooding), radon gas hazard, ground stability issues and the property's proximity to any waste sites or other potentially contaminated sites.

Water authority searches. To find out if any public drains on the property might affect future building works. If there's a mains drain running under where you envisaged building an extension, that would put an end to this plan.

Optional and location specific searches. These vary across the country. In Cornwall, for example, a tin-mining search is often included as an additional search. No one wants their property collapsing into a disused mine.

Title register and title plan at the Land Registry. This is to confirm the current ownership of the property and the property boundary. Note: If you are buying a flat with the loft space above, do not assume you own this loft space (even if you have sole access). Often it will not have been demised

to anyone. Ask your solicitor to check if this is the case. It
should be possible to purchase this attic space from the other
property owners in the block for a reasonably small amount
provided they are willing to sell. However, this could be a
long process.

Planning consents. If the property has been altered, your
solicitor will check the necessary permissions have been
obtained and that the work was signed off by building control.
It's also worth checking to see if planning permission has
been turned down in the past. You can find this information
on the local authority's website.

Restrictive covenants. For example, some properties can
only be purchased by the over 55s.

What's included in the sale. Some sellers will strip the
place bare (in one notable case, even the light bulbs were
taken). Others will happily leave blinds, sofas, washing
machines, beds, etc. Your solicitor will provide you a list of
what will be included. You might not agree with everything
on the list, but you need to be flexible. Remember, these are
short-term niggles; don't let them ruin months of searching
and tricky negotiations.

Guarantees. These may be for building work that's been
carried out or for such things as a replacement boiler. New
builds less than ten years old should come with a guarantee
too.

Legal charges. Your solicitor will also check there is no
other legal charge against the property. In other words, that
no one else (or no other lender) has asserted their rights to
the property.

Right of way. Some properties will have public footpaths
that run through the garden; others will allow people to
access their property via, for example, their neighbour's
drive.

Disputes. The seller will have filled in a property questionnaire, which also asks about past and present disputes. If there has been a dispute with a neighbour, a little more probing is probably a good idea. Having an unpleasant neighbour could ruin your enjoyment of the property.

The lease. Your solicitor will check the lease is in order. They should highlight any issues such as excessive ground rent/service charges, a short lease and leasehold covenants. Note: If I am planning on buying a share of freehold of a property, I ask my solicitor to check the leases of all the properties in the block. If any have high current or future ground rents, I know their participation in purchasing the freehold will be expensive. As such they are less likely to participate, which means I will be less likely to be able to purchase the freehold.

Finding a good solicitor

Nothing beats a personal recommendation. Ask friends or family members for recommendations. Also, it's the individual solicitor that counts, not the company. If you get a recommendation, make sure you are allocated the same solicitor. Google reviews are another way of finding a good solicitor. Also, certain mortgage offers (especially for first-time buyers) will come with reduced-price conveyancing - this is definitely a viable option. Estate agents will be able to make recommendations too - but you should probably avoid this, as there's a possible conflict of interest. After all, the estate agents are being paid by the seller not you. Also, The Law Society's website has a solicitor-finding tool: https://www.lawsociety.org.uk/

Note: Most solicitors will charge between £600 and £1,400 +VAT for conveyancing, depending on the level of complexity.

Review your mortgage

Before you book a survey, call your mortgage advisor informing them of the exact amount you need to borrow (based on the accepted offer). Ask them to see if there are better options available that you will definitely be able to access. Remember, loyalty doesn't pay in the mortgage market - ditch your mortgage-in-principle lender if that will save you money.

Which survey is right for you?

There are various levels of survey, from a simple valuation to a full structural survey. The one you choose will probably depend on your budget, your knowledge and your attitude to risk. But, more cautious buyers may choose a full structural survey, especially if the property is in a poor state of repair. Note: all lenders will require you to get a survey before they lend the money.

These are the three main types of property survey:

Valuation report. This isn't a proper survey, as the inspector is only there to ascertain that the property is worth what the purchaser has agreed to pay. The 'surveyor' is unlikely to pick up on anything you haven't already noticed. This type of survey is often used with remortgages. Expect to pay in the region of £300 +VAT for this survey.

Homebuyer's report. This is a proper survey and will highlight problems such as woodworm, subsidence or rot. The report will also make suggestions as to what remedial works need to be undertaken. In addition, this survey should flag changes to the property that would have required building-control sign-off, such as the creation of a through-lounge. This allows you to check that the relevant sign-offs have been obtained. The report also includes rebuild costs, which is useful when you're getting buildings-insurance quotes. However, this is a sight-only report – they won't lift carpets or floorboards. You have been warned. Expect to pay in the region of £500 +VAT for this survey.

Full structural survey. This is the most comprehensive survey you can get. The inspector will carry out a full inspection of the property internally and externally. As with the homebuyer's survey, it will flag issues and suggest possible remedies. This survey is far more likely to unearth more problems. The loft space, for example, will be inspected.

Expect to pay in the region of £750 +VAT for this survey. Remember: New builds come with a 10-year guarantee. Make sure you get a professional to produce a snagging list.

Survey results

In our increasingly litigious society, surveyor's reports are peppered with legal-speak. This is a line from a recent report I read: "Although no woodworm was evident, you are advised to employ a specialist company to carry out a full woodworm inspection." The report also advised the buyer to get specialists to inspect the electrics, gas and the roof/chimney. Even the best-maintained older property will sound like it's about to collapse. Don't be afraid of the report. Instead, focus on the following:

Cracks. Are there any significant cracks in the walls? If there are, that might be a sign of subsidence. This can be expensive to repair, as it will involve underpinning the property. Bowing or bulging external walls should be investigated further too.

Boiler. If it's more than eight years old, it may well need replacing. This is an expensive job too.

Electrics. Are there enough power sockets? How new is the fuse box? Rewiring a property is an expensive business.

Roof. Is there underfelt? Are there loose or cracked slates/tiles? Is the lead flashing in good condition (this sits between the brickwork and the slates/tiles)? Is the guttering in a good state of repair? Is there any sign of the timbers bowing?

Chimney. These can be expensive to repair, as scaffolding is needed. Check the report clears it of any defects.

Damp. Is there any significant damp?

Trees. Are there any large trees near the property that could cause it structural issues? Tree roots can destroy drains and damage a property's foundations.

Dry rot. If this is detected and is extensive, you may need to rebuild the affected areas.

Windows. Are they in a good state of repair? If they are wooden are there any signs of wood rot? Are all the double-glazed units free from mist? If the windows/doors are new, they should come with a FENSA certificate, which aims to guarantee quality. There's a nationwide database of these certificates: https://www.fensa.org.uk/fensa-certificate

Woodworm. If this comes up in the report, does the seller have any guarantees in place for remedial work previously undertaken.

Drains. Are these free from blockages and in good working order?

Japanese Knotweed. If this is found at the property or nearby, your lender may withdraw your mortgage offer.

If anything significant does come up in the survey, it should be re-inspected by a third party. Ask your estate agent to arrange for specialist tradespeople to quote for repairing these issues. These quotes should be free. Once you know how much the remedial work will cost, you could consider asking the seller to reduce the price to reflect these costs. But if it's your dream home, be careful not to rock the boat too much. What's a few thousand pounds spread over the years you might live there?

Note: Your lender will look carefully at the survey results too and you will not receive a final mortgage offer until they have done so. Sometimes, lenders will withhold a proportion of the mortgage until certain works are completed.

Mortgage offer

Assuming your survey results are satisfactory and the property searches haven't unearthed anything untoward, you will receive a mortgage offer. Most mortgage offers are valid for six months, so that's how long you have to complete on the property. Although, of course, most people won't want things to drag out that long.

Indemnity insurance

Sometimes the seller may not be able to provide all the paperwork required to satisfy your lender. For example, the property title may be defective or alterations may have been made without planning permission. This is where indemnity insurance can help. In simple terms, indemnity insurance insures buyers against possible future legal problems or local council action. Indemnity insurance is a one-off payment policy that lasts forever and is tied to the property. This means if you ever sell the property it can be passed to the new owner.

Always question the need for this policy, as there is sometimes a workaround. If there isn't, such policies are often a good option. Who should pay is a hotly-contested question. On balance, it should probably be the seller, but splitting the costs may be a good way of helping close the deal. The cost of such policies ranges from less than £100 for missing FENSA certificates to hundreds of pounds for missing planning permission documents.

As this is specialist insurance, your solicitor will contact specialist brokers to obtain quotes.

Exchange of contracts

An exchange of contracts involves two copies of a contract of sale being signed. Each party will retain one copy. Your solicitor will send you a copy of the contract to sign and get witnessed. The witness should not be a relative or have any financial interest in the property. Please note:

- Both parties need to agree the exchange and completion dates prior to the exchange of contracts. The sooner both parties – the buyer and the seller – can agree an exchange date the better. Having a deadline to work towards always focuses the mind. The more protracted the property-transaction process, the greater the chance of an unsuccessful outcome. Remember, prior to exchange either party can pull out of the transaction at any time and for any reason.
- Although it is technically possible to exchange and complete on the same day, I would not recommend it as it adds extra layers of stress. Standard practice is for there to be a seven-day to 28-day gap between exchange and completion.

- Exchange should only take place once your mortgage offer has been approved and your solicitor is satisfied with the property search outcomes, etc.
- Normally a 10% deposit is required in order to exchange contracts, although this is often waived (or can be lower). If you don't have this amount in cash, speak to your solicitor in advance.
- Once you have exchanged contracts, the transaction becomes legally binding. If you pull out after exchange, you could be sued for breach of contract. So, only sign the contract if you are 100% certain you want to proceed.
- Buildings insurance will be a condition of your mortgage. The amount of cover must be at least enough to cover the outstanding mortgage. However, covering the full potential rebuild costs makes more sense. Do not automatically buy this insurance through your lender - although some will charge a small fee if you don't. You should be able to get a much better deal on the open market. You can find all the price comparison websites here: https://www.moneysavingexpert.com/
- Note: If you're buying a freehold property, you're responsible for arranging your buildings insurance. If it's a leasehold property, the freeholder will be responsible for this - and you will be expected to pay them your share of the buildings-insurance costs.
- Some lenders will ask you to take out life insurance too. This is to cover the cost of the mortgage should the owner/owners die. The most inexpensive option is term insurance. Effectively you insure your life for a set number of years for a set amount of money. For

example, £300,000 for the next 25 years. Joint life policies pay out on the death of one of the policyholders. Shop around for the best rates: https://www.lifeinsurancecover.co.uk/

Once contracts have been exchanged, your solicitor will prepare the transfer document that transfers the title of the property from the seller to the buyer. They will also ensure the mortgage documents are signed and finalised, so that the money is available on the agreed completion date.

Top tip: Once you have exchanged, you can be certain of the completion date. Start making plans for that date - there's lots of work to do!

Completion

This is a hugely exciting (and busy) day as you'll get the keys to your new property. Please note, however, that most properties complete on a Friday and sometimes you'll effectively be in a queue. So, don't expect completion to happen first thing. Instead, keep in regular contact with your solicitor. After all, the squeaky wheel gets the oil. Some other things to bear in mind:

- Your mortgage lender transfers the money to your solicitor, who then transfers this money to the seller's solicitor, who then transfers this money to the seller. So, it's a bit of a merry-go-round. And sometimes things go wrong. If the money hasn't gone through by 3pm, you will probably have to wait until the next working day to complete.
- Once completion has taken place, you will need to collect the key (usually from the estate agent).
- On completion day you will also need to pay all additional costs, most notably stamp duty and your

legal fees. Your solicitor will send you a statement of completion which will detail all the costs incurred.

- On that day, your solicitor will notify the Land Registry of the transfer of ownership. The property deeds will then be sent to your mortgage lender, who will retain them until the mortgage has been paid off or you sell the property.

Scotland is different (most would say in a good way)
If you see a property you want to buy, the first thing you do is file a "Note of Interest" with the estate agent. The agent is then legally obliged to keep you abreast of any changes such as a change of price. The vendor will then decide a "closing date" - by noon of that day, you will need to have filed your 'best and final offer' with the agent (this is the same as a sealed bid). The winning bid will invariably be the highest. If you're buying a property in Scotland, more research into property prices is crucial. Although buyers are not meant to see the amount other potential buyers bid, there have been cases when buyers have discovered their bid far exceeded the next best bid. This is always going to leave a bitter taste in your mouth.

A common misconception is that the "winner" now has a legal obligation to buy the property. This is untrue. The next phase is for the seller's solicitor to send your solicitor a "qualified acceptance", which means they accept the offer depending on certain conditions (such as the date you want to collect the keys and move in). The seller's solicitor and your solicitor will then send each other "missives" negotiating these conditions. These letters aim to hammer out the final terms of the sale. Once the missives are accepted and both you and the seller agree on the terms, you have a legally-binding contract. As with all legally-binding contracts, pulling out at this stage is inadvisable as you would be liable to pay the seller significant damages. The final stage is known as "settlement". This is when the buyer pays the seller the agreed price on the date that's been agreed in the contract.

What if things go wrong?
Sometimes, through no fault of your own, a purchase will fall through. This can be a very painful experience, especially if you've set your heart on living there. It can be expensive too, as you may have incurred costs, such as legal and surveyor costs.

But, there are countless tales of people who lose out on a property only to secure a better one a few months later. Buying property can feel like a war of attrition. But, if you stay the course, invariably it'll prove to be a war worth winning. So:

- Dust yourself down, and get back on the bike. Remember, you can't change the past, but you can change the future.
- Keep on good terms with the estate agent. They make money through successful sales. If they think you are a good buyer, they will want to sell you another property. Plus, they will know the kind of property you like.
- Get back in contact with other estate agents in the area - they need to know you're back in the market. Also, don't forget other property-finding options such as leafleting.
- Don't fall out with the seller, even if they have pulled out at the last moment. They may have had a good reason for this. And, who knows, that could change

in a few months' time. You need to be ready to pounce.

If you have a complaint
The estate agent. If you think you have been unfairly treated by an estate agent, you should initially make this complaint to the manager of the branch. You should do this in writing, setting out the act or omission you believe has occurred. Ideally you should also detail how you would like them to resolve your complaint. Follow up any verbal conversations in writing, making a note of the date, time and the name of the person you spoke to. If you're not happy with the way your complaint has been dealt with, you could consider raising it with the The Property Ombudsman: https://www.tpos.co.uk/
Your solicitor. As above, you should initially make the complaint to your solicitor. You may want to include the senior partner of the firm. If you're unhappy with how they have dealt with your complaint, you can take your complaint to the Solicitors Regulation Authority: https://www.sra.org.uk
Your mortgage lender/advisor. The first step is to send your complaint to the lender or mortgage advisor in writing. Financial Conduct Authority rules require them to send a written acknowledgement of your complaint within five business days. If they cannot make a final decision on your complaint after a month, they must notify you. Again, if you're unhappy with how your complaint has been dealt with, you can escalate your grievance, in this instance with the Financial Ombudsman: https://www.financial-ombudsman.org.uk/

Paying your mortgage

Once you become a homeowner, paying your monthly mortgage has to be your priority. However, anyone can fall on hard times - thousands of properties are repossessed every year. This tends to happen when a homeowner falls into arrears (i.e. they owe the lender one or more interest payment). If you find yourself struggling financially, there are a few key steps you should take:

- If it's likely you will be unable to make a mortgage payment, notify your lender in advance. Most will act with compassion and will want to work with you to find a solution.

- The Government, under certain circumstances, will help. Their Support for Mortgage Interest (SMI) scheme will pay some of the mortgage interest. If you're eligible, the Government will pay the interest on the first £200,000 of your outstanding mortgage. But, they pay at their interest rate, not that of your lender. The eligibility criteria is pretty steep and likely to change. Follow this link to find the latest details: https://www.gov.uk/support-for-mortgage-interest

Mortgage Payment Protection Insurance (MPPI)

For most new homeowners, the monthly mortgage payment will probably be their largest outgoing. And, if you fall behind on your mortgage payments, you risk being repossessed. This is where MPPI steps in. There are three main types of MPPI:

Unemployment. This is the cheapest option and will only pay out if you are made redundant.

Accident and sickness. This policy will pay out in the case of a serious accident or if you have a long-term illness.

Accident, sickness and unemployment. This is the most expensive, as it covers the most scenarios.

The concept of MPPI is a good one, but there are definitely some caveats:

- Anyone with a pre-existing medical condition could find their policy is declined, subject to a premium hike or comes with added clauses.
- If you're self-employed, MPPI is probably a no go.
- Most policies will pay out for a maximum of two years; others are limited to 12 months. However, some long-term illnesses can last a lifetime.
- Mental-health issues are not considered long-term illnesses by most insurers. This strikes me as somewhat backwards.
- You will be unable to claim until you have been off work for a certain number of days. This waiting period varies from policy to policy, and can range from 30 to 180 days. Most young people who are made redundant tend to find a new job reasonably swiftly. Usually, the cheaper the MPPI policy, the longer the waiting period.
- You can choose the level of cover you require. It could just cover your mortgage payments. But you could choose it to cover your whole salary or 150% of your mortgage payments. Needless to say, the higher the cover, the higher the monthly policy premium.
- Finally, as with financial products, shop around for the best deal. Do not buy MPPI from your mortgage lender – it's highly unlikely their quote will be the lowest.

Making a will

Unfortunately, we're all mortal. And, if you don't have a will, you should consider writing one once you become a homeowner. Some things to consider:

- If someone dies without a valid will, they become what is known as "intestate". Their estate must be shared out according to the rules of intestacy. If you would like to see how this could affect you, follow this link: https://www.gov.uk/inherits-someone-dies-without-will

- If you have purchased the property as a co-owner, and you opted for Tenancy in Common, you have the right to leave your share of the property to whomever you choose. You will need to specify this in your will.

- If you just need a fairly basic will, there's a charity will-writing scheme. Every November, participating solicitors waive their fee for writing a basic will. Instead, they invite clients to make a voluntary donation to Will Aid. The charity suggests this donation should be in the region of £100 for a single will. For more details, follow this link: https://www.willaid.org.uk/

Part 5 - Moving into your first property

Planning for the move

Moving home is the best of times; moving home is the worst of times. There's nothing more exciting than moving home. But the sheer amount of work involved can be daunting. The best advice I can give is to start early (but not before you have exchanged contracts). Here are some things you need to consider before the day of the move:

Transportation. What you choose will depend on how much stuff you have to move. If you think you need to employ professional movers, try to get a few quotes from reputable local companies. If it's a small move, a man and van might be the most cost-effective option. Counterintuitively, a "man [or woman] and van" is often cheaper than hiring a van. That's because you don't have to be insured to drive the vehicle. If you want to drive yourself, get quotes from Travelsupermarket or sign up with Zipcar.

Insurance. If you have contents insurance, check it covers your possessions in transit. If you don't, consider arranging this.

Parking. Find out if there is parking near the property. Some councils will allow you to book a parking bay outside the property for the day of the move. They will, of course, charge you for this service.

If you're currently renting. Notify your landlord/landlady of your move-out date.

Book time off work. Most employers will allow employees at least one day off for moving. But you will need to book this in advance. Also, call in some favours - try to find people who will help you on the day. This is when you find out who your real friends are!

Childcare. If you have children, try to find someone who can look after them for the day. The same goes for pets.

Redirect your mail. This is so you don't miss important documents. It should also prevent your personal details falling into the wrong hands and you becoming a victim of fraud. You can, for a fee, redirect your mail for three, six or 12 months. Google "Royal Mail redirection" for details.

Change your address. As well as redirecting your mail, it's vital you change your address on anything that could affect your credit score. These include:

- Mobile-phone contract.
- Electoral roll.
- Bank accounts.
- Building-society accounts.
- Credit cards.
- Store cards.

Have a look through your purse/wallet too - that usually unearths a few you haven't thought of. Notify the following of your change of address too:

- Driving licence/Vehicle registration document (V5C)
- HMRC.
- Travel insurance.
- Memberships (e.g. the gym).
- ISA provider/providers.
- Pension provider/providers.
- Doctor/dentist (although you may need to find new ones).
- And, of course, friends and family.

Packing. If you've been living in the same place for a number of years, start packing as soon as possible. As a rule of thumb, order twice as many packing boxes as you think you'll need. Label each box on the top and the side.

Tape furniture fittings to the furniture. You can buy moving kits online from, for example, https://www.packingboxes.co.uk/

Keep pile, sell pile, charity-shop pile and dump pile. One of the joys of moving is that cathartic feeling of having just undertaken a massive clear out. You discover prized possessions you'd long forgotten about, and you can offload those purchases you shouldn't have bought in the first place. Now is the time to be ruthless. It's a great opportunity to unburden yourself from the shackles of owning too much "stuff". Some stuff you can sell on eBay. There's also a neat app, Ziffit, that allows you to scan numerous items and sell them as a "job lot". Charity shops are always happy to receive donations (some will even collect larger items of furniture/white goods) - choose them over landfill.

Storage. Try not to put stuff in storage, even if you think it's for the short term. Storage is expensive, and people tend to put off getting things out of storage, so the costs add up. Just 50 sq ft of storage space will cost you in the region of £2,000 a year. However, if you have to store some stuff, try Storemates and Stashbee - they are the AirBnB of the storage world (and much cheaper than traditional storage companies).

Valuables/breakables. Keep these separate if you can and move them yourself. If, for example, you're living with your parents, move your valuables at a later date.

Don't forget the loft. Or the garage or the garden shed, for that matter. These can be messy jobs - don't leave them to the last minute. Properties should be left completely empty - your landlord/landlady can charge you for the removal of anything you leave.

Ask the seller questions. You should have received the completed seller's questionnaire, that should include such things as utility providers, management company details, etc. Have another look at this and see if there are any unanswered questions. If there are, ask the estate agent for the seller's contact details (which, after exchange, should be fine). Here are some suggestions:

- If there's a thermostat, where is it?
- Where's the stop cock for the water?
- Do they have instruction manuals for the appliances? If so, ask them to leave them.
- Where were the kitchen units bought from?
- Where were the kitchen/bathroom tiles bought from? Are there any spare tiles? If so, ask them to leave them.
- Ask them to leave any half-used pots of paint.
- Ask them to leave any guarantee certificates.
- Ask them about parking restrictions.

The day of the move
Moving out. If you've been renting, take time to empty and clean the property thoroughly. Take lots of photos too. This should increase your chances of getting your deposit back in full. In addition, make sure you notify:

- The utility providers - water, gas and electricity. For the latter two, you'll need to take a final meter reading too.
- Your broadband provider.
- Your landline provider.
- The council - for council tax purposes.

Call/email your solicitor first thing. Chances are they will be completing on other properties too. Try to make sure they prioritise yours.

Keys. Check who will have these (it's usually the estate agent). When you arrive at the property, check you have keys for everything including for the windows, the back door and any outbuildings.

Overnight bag. Keep everything you need for your first night separate (i.e. not in a packing box). Pack a picnic and lots of snacks too. And, of course, make sure the kettle and mugs are accessible.

Cleaning items. These will be essential. You know the kind of thing: dustpan and brush, cloths, bin bags, bleach, etc.

Tool kit. You may have to assemble furniture. If you don't have one, you can buy a basic one on Amazon for less than £20.

Tea, coffee and biscuits. Whether you have friends and family helping you or professional movers, these will be welcomed by everyone. And, if you want a job done well, treating people with kindness and respect works wonders.

The first day in your new home
Many first-time buyers find wandering around their new home for the first time deflating. An empty property feels unloved and, often, pretty shabby. It takes time for a property to become a home - it's the memories that make it such. If you don't feel that connection straight away, give it time. Once you repaint a few rooms and install your possessions, things will look up too.

I've tried to avoid talking too much about my experiences while writing this book. It was a far different era - and this book is mainly for a younger generation. But I will say this: the first day in my first property was one of the best days of my life. The sellers had left a bottle of champagne, two glasses and a card (something I have repeated every time I have sold a property); I had no sofa or bed (just a mattress); I was completely skint; I was exhausted - and I could not have been any happier. All the hard work had paid off. Myself and Bertie (a friend who helped me move in - thank you Bertie!) sat on the mattress, listening to music and sipping champagne. The decorating could wait.

Your first week of home ownership

Parking permits. If you need a parking permit, find out what documentation you require as evidence you're now a resident. You will need to apply for your parking permit online, on the council's website. Do not expect a speedy turnaround.

Council tax. Provide the council with the date you moved in and with details of everyone who will be living at the property.

Doctor/dentist. Try to register with a local dentist/doctor. Also, find out the address of your nearest A&E department (just in case).

Change the front-door locks. Especially if the property has been tenanted. That's because far more people will have had access to the keys.

Reducing your property outgoings

Running a property can be an expensive business. Here are some tips to reduce your outgoings:

Utilities (gas and electricity). You should sign up to Moneysavingexpert's cheap energy club:
https://www.moneysavingexpert.com/cheapenergyclub
They will ensure you are always on the cheapest tariff without you having to do anything.

Reduce energy consumption. If you're buying new appliances such as fridges and freezers, look for the most energy efficient. A sticker on each appliance shows a series of colour co-ordinated bars from A+++ to G. A+++ is the most energy efficient. Also, make sure you install energy saving light bulbs and don't leave your television on standby. **Water bills.** Water companies are regional monopolies, so you can't switch supplier. However, you can reduce your water consumption. And, given that most properties now have water meters, that's well worth doing - for your pocket and the environment. Here are some tips:

- Change your showerhead. Water-efficient showerheads force air into the water stream through a small hole. The water and air then mix in the showerhead, resulting in the power of a conventional shower, while minimising water usage.
- Water-efficient appliances. If you're planning on changing your washing machine or dishwasher, look for the Waterwise checkmark, which will rate the appliance for water consumption. And make sure they're always full before you turn them on, using the eco setting (obviously).
- Fit tap aerators. These can be fitted to, for example, kitchen taps. If you tend to fill the sink when you're washing up, these are of limited use. But, if you keep the tap flowing, they will reduce your water consumption.
- Turn the tap off. People who leave the tap on when brushing their teeth waste six litres of water a minute. Ouch!
- Fix that dripping tap. Or waste 5,500 litres of water a year. It's surprisingly easy to change the rubber washers in a tap. YouTube is awash (no pun intended) with videos that will show you how.

Broadband. As most bills have continued to rise, the cost of broadband has continued to fall - that's the impact of a truly competitive market. Depending on where you live, you may be able to get broadband without having a landline. For the best deals, head to one of the price-comparison websites, such as uSwitch. As an aside, some broadband providers offer bundled packages, such as mobile SIM only and broadband, which are often very competitive.

Television. Many households are paying hundreds of pounds each month on expensive TV packages. If you enjoy watching television, it might be worth rethinking what you're paying for and whether it's worth it.

Council tax. If just one person lives in your property (or just one adult) you may be entitled to a 25% discount. So, if this is the case, contact your local council as soon as possible. You're also entitled to a 25% discount if the person you live with is medically certified as having a "severe mental impairment" (e.g. Parkinson's) or has had a stroke. Again, if this is the case, inform your local council. In addition, it's thought that 400,000 households in England and Scotland are in the wrong council-tax band. If you think your property has been overvalued, you can apply to have this changed. To check sold prices of properties on your street, head to nethouseprices.com. You can then check this against council valuations (for Scotland head to: https: saa.gov.uk; for England it's: gov.uk/council-tax-bands). If there's a discrepancy, write to your council. But only if your property has been overvalued.

Gardens. Some garden costs are unavoidable, but it's definitely possible to save considerable sums by taking cuttings, planting seeds and scouring the Internet for the best value tools. Also, many people give away unwanted plants, pots and garden tools on websites such as Freecycle.

Household furnishings. These can also be purchased or sourced for free in the same manner. But, if you are buying from new, spend the money up front to save buying twice. Also, always consider upcycling and restoring existing items.

Cash in case of emergencies
Try to build up some savings. Unexpected costs can hit homeowners hard. And short-term loans are expensive.

Final thoughts
You will only be a first-time buyer once. Try to enjoy the process and savour that final moment of success. And don't forget to thank everyone who helped you along the way. Paths often cross in the future. So, why not send a card and chocolates to the following:

- The estate agent (who may well find you another property in the future).
- Your mortgage advisor (who may help you remortgage when your fixed-term mortgage comes to an end).
- Your friends and family members who helped.

Requests from the author
- Firstly, thank you for buying this book.
- Secondly, please review this book on Amazon or Good Reads. If you've enjoyed reading this book (or you didn't, but you learned lots), please leave a positive review.
- Finally, if you spotted any mistakes or omissions, please email me (nedbrowne@hotmail.com), so I can amend/improve future editions. You will, of course, receive a free copy of any new edition.

Appendix

Advance. The amount your lender agrees to lend you. In other words, the amount of the mortgage loan.

100% mortgage. A mortgage that does not require the borrower to have a deposit. As the name would suggest, the loan covers 100% of the property purchase price.

Annual Percentage Rate (APR). This is the official rate used for borrowing. It's expressed as a yearly percentage.

Arrears. When you fall behind with your mortgage payment, you are said to be in arrears.

Asking price. How much the seller has stated they want for their property.

Auction. A publicly held sale at which property is sold to the highest bidder.

Base rate. This is the rate of interest set by the Bank of England.

Building Control. All major building work has to be signed off by Building Control. They will issue certificates for all work that meets the required standards.

Buildings insurance. This insurance covers the cost of repairing damage to the physical structure of a property in the event of damage or theft.

Buy To Let (BTL). This is when an investor purchases a property in order to let it out to tenants.

Buying agent. These agents can help you find a property and negotiate the best price for that property.

Capped mortgage. This is a type of variable-rate mortgage that has an interest-rate ceiling (or cap) beyond which your payments cannot rise.

Cohabitation agreement. This agreement allows you to document how you will split your property (and, optionally, contents, personal belongings, debts, savings and other assets) if your relationship breaks down.

Communal area. The parts of a property that the tenants have a right to use in common with other tenants. The freeholder is normally responsible for these areas.

Completion. This is the final step in the legal process of transferring the ownership of a property.

Contents insurance. This insurance covers the cost of damage to, or loss of, an individual's personal possessions when they are located within that individual's home.

Conveyancing. The process of transferring the legal ownership of property (or land) from one person to another.

Conveyancing solicitor. A professional who undertakes the act of conveyancing on behalf of the seller or buyer.

Council tax. A tax levied on households by local authorities, based on the estimated value of a property and the number of people living in it.

Credit score. A credit score is a statistical number that evaluates a consumer's creditworthiness based on their credit history. Most credit scores range from 300 to 850 - the higher your score the better.

Deposit. In the world of property, a deposit can mean two things. Firstly, it's the lump sum of money you save to help finance your property. For example, 10% of the asking price.

Deposit. A deposit can also refer to a sum of money that is paid by the buyer on exchange of contracts.

Electoral roll. An official list of the people in a district who are entitled to vote in an election.

Energy Performance Certificate (EPC). A certificate that shows you how energy efficient the property currently is and how efficient it has the potential to become. An EPC gives a property an energy efficiency rating from A (most efficient) to G (least efficient).

Environmental search. This provides details of the past uses of the land in the vicinity of the property and whether such past uses are likely to cause a potential hazard.

Equity. The difference between the value of the property and the outstanding mortgage. E.g. If a property was worth £450,000 and the outstanding mortgage was £300,000, the equity would be £150,000.

Exchange. Exchange of contracts is when the two conveyancing solicitors swap signed contracts. At this point, the agreement to buy the property becomes legally binding.

Financial Ombudsman. The Financial Ombudsman Service settles individual disputes between consumers and businesses that provide financial services.

Fixed-rate mortgage. A type of mortgage where the interest rate is fixed for a set period of time. The interest rate is usually fixed for two or five years.

Floorplan. A scale diagram of the arrangement and dimensions of rooms in the property. Many will include the total floor area of the property.

Freehold. The ultimate (and therefore best) title in property. A freehold property includes the building and the land upon which the building sits.

Freeholder. A freeholder is a company or a person who owns the freehold of the building. Freeholders are usually responsible for the repair and maintenance of the exterior and common parts of the building.

Full structural survey. Also known as a building survey, this is the most comprehensive report on the condition of a residential property. This is mainly used for older properties in a poor state of repair. The surveyor will inspect all accessible parts of a property for any potential issues.

Gazump. This is when someone makes a higher offer for a property after someone else's offer has already been accepted. The person who makes the higher offer ends up buying the property.

Gazunder. This is when the buyer lowers the price that has been previously agreed by both the buyer and the seller. This invariably occurs just before the exchange of contracts.

Generation rent. The generation of young adults who, because of high property prices, live in rented accommodation and are regarded as having little chance of ever becoming homeowners.

Ground rent. Rent paid under the terms of a lease by the leaseholder of a property to the freeholder.

Guarantor. A person who agrees to pay the mortgage loan if you cannot.

Guarantor mortgage. This is any mortgage where a guarantor effectively underwrites the loan. In simple terms, you find someone (usually a family member) to agree to pay the loan if you cannot.

Homebuyer's report. This is a mid-range survey. It sits between a valuation report and a full structural survey.

Indemnity insurance. Indemnity insurance insures buyers against possible future legal problems or local council action. This insurance may have to be purchased if the seller cannot provide all the paperwork required to satisfy your lender.

Independent Financial Advisor (IFA). Independent mortgage advisors provide unbiased, impartial advice as they advise on financial products offered by a range of different financial organisations.

Inflation (Consumer Price Index - CPI). This measures the average change from month to month in the prices of goods and services purchased by most households in the UK. The Government uses the CPI as the basis for its inflation target.

Inflation (Retail Price Index - RPI). This measures the average change from month to month in the prices of goods and services purchased by most households in the UK. Unlike CPI, RPI does include housing costs.

Interest rate. The amount of interest a borrower has to pay is calculated by the interest rate set by the lender. It is expressed as a percentage.

Interest-only mortgage. A mortgage where your monthly payments only cover the mortgage-loan interest (and do not contribute to repaying the outstanding capital).

Japanese knotweed. A pernicious plant that can grow through tarmac, destroy drains, and can grow under and through foundations.

Joint tenancy. A type of joint ownership. If one of the

owners dies, their share of the property automatically goes to the surviving owner/owners.

Land Registry. The Government department created in 1862 that's responsible for registering the ownership of land and property in England and Wales.

Law Society. An independent professional body for solicitors in England and Wales.

Lease. A contract by which one party conveys a property to another party for a specified time. It outlines the length of time, the conditions and the ground rent and service charges payable.

Leasehold. A leasehold property entitles the leaseholder to live at that property for a specified amount of time according to the terms of a lease. The land upon which the property sits is owned by the freeholder.

Leasehold covenant. Leasehold covenants are promises made between a landlord and tenant, and are normally included in the lease. Responsibilities are placed on a landlord or tenant to do what the covenants state. For example, a leasehold covenant may state you cannot use your property as a holiday let.

Leaseholder. A leaseholder is a person who is allowed to use a property according to the terms of a lease.

Lifetime (Individual Savings Account) ISA. Also known as LISAs, lifetime ISAs allow people to save for their first home (or retirement). All interest is earned free from tax. Moreover, the Government will boost your savings by 25% of what you pay in, up to a set limit, every tax year.

Listed building. A building is listed when it is of special architectural or historic interest. Listed buildings have extra legal protection within the planning system.

Loan To Value (LTV). This refers to the maximum, as a percentage of the property's value, the lender is willing to lend. So, for example, if the maximum Loan To Value was 90% and the property was priced at £300,000, the mortgage lender would loan a maximum of £270,000 (i.e. 90% of £300,000).

Local Authority search. A search instructed by a conveyancing solicitor to ascertain, for example, if the property is a listed building, or if it's located in a conservation area or smoke-control zone.

Management company. This is the company that is responsible for maintaining a block of flats. It may have been set up by the freeholder. However, if the leaseholders are also the freeholders (i.e. they own the share of freehold), or if the leaseholders have the Right to Manage, the leaseholders will run the management company.

Marriage value. If a person wants to extend their lease and the current lease is less than 80 years, the freeholder is entitled to an additional payment known as the "Marriage Value". In simple terms, this is 50% of the uplift in the property value after the lease extension.

Mortgage advisor. A professional who gives you financial advice and support on different mortgage options.

Mortgage in principle. A certificate issued by a lender that says, in principle, how much money they are willing to lend you.

Mortgage offer. This is when your lender approves your mortgage loan. Most mortgage offers are valid for six months.

Mortgage Payment Protection Insurance (MPPI). An insurance policy that pays your mortgage should you become ill or lose your job.

Mortgage term. This is the length of time the loan is required. The most common mortgage term for a first-time buyer is 25 years.

Mortgage underwriter. The person responsible for approving or rejecting your mortgage application.

Negative equity. When the property is worth less than the outstanding mortgage.

Off-plan. Buying off-plan is when you purchase a property that has yet to be built.

Offer. The amount the buyer offers to pay the seller for the property. Most offers are put in writing to the estate agent selling the property.

Offset mortgage. A mortgage that links the borrower's mortgage account and savings account. Any savings you hold are offset against mortgage-interest payments, so you only pay interest on your mortgage balance minus your savings balance.

Payday loan. A relatively small amount of money lent at a high rate of interest on the agreement that it will be repaid when the borrower next gets paid.

Planning permission. This is issued by local authorities. Developers and property owners are normally not allowed to build new properties or make extensive changes to existing properties without planning permission.

Private sale. When a property is sold directly to a buyer. In other words, there is no third party (such as an estate agent) involved.

Property chain. A property chain is when a property purchase depends on one or more additional transactions taking place.

Property Ombudsman. The Property Ombudsman provides a dispute-resolution service for consumers and property agents.

Repayment mortgage. A mortgage where your monthly payments cover the interest and a part of the capital.

Repossession. When the lender takes possession of a property when the borrower has defaulted on their mortgage payments.

Restrictive covenant. A restriction placed on how a property can be used. For example, some properties can only be purchased by the over 55s.

Right of way. The legal right, established by usage or grant, to pass along a specific route through grounds or property belonging to another.

Right To Manage (RTM). RTM lets some leasehold property owners take over management of the building - even without the agreement of the landlord.

Sealed bids. A method of selling a property that requires all bidders (prospective buyers) to simultaneously submit sealed bids to the estate agent so that no bidder knows how much the other prospective buyers have offered. The highest bidder will usually be declared the winner.

Service charges. These are paid to the freeholder to cover the cost of such things as maintaining communal gardens, electricity bills for communal areas, buildings insurance, repair and maintenance of exterior walls, windows and roofs.

Share of freehold. When the leaseholders in a block of flats have acquired a shared ownership of the freehold title. Usually the freehold title is registered in the name of a company in which the flat owners will be shareholders. So, each leaseholder owns a share of the freehold too.

Solicitors' Regulation Authority. The Solicitors Regulation Authority (SRA) is the regulatory body for solicitors in England and Wales.

Sold (Subject To Contract - STC). This describes the time between an offer being accepted and the exchange of contracts.

Stamp duty. Stamp Duty Land Tax (SDLT) is payable if you buy a property or land over a certain price in England and Northern Ireland. In Scotland you pay Land and Buildings Transaction Tax. In Wales you pay Land Transaction Tax.

Standard-variable-rate mortgage. A mortgage where the interest you pay on your monthly mortgage payments can go up or down, depending on where your mortgage lender decides to set its standard variable rate.

Student loan. A type of loan designed to help students pay for post-secondary education.

Subsidence. This occurs when the ground underneath your house sinks. Bad subsidence can cause significant structural damage to a property. Homes suffering from subsidence may have to be underpinned.

Support for Mortgage Interest (SMI). A Government scheme designed to help homeowners pay the interest on their loans, if they are struggling to make the payments. It offers limited support and the eligibility criteria are very strict.

Survey. A generic term to describe all property surveys, including valuation reports, homebuyer's reports and full structural surveys.

Tenants in common. A type of joint ownership. If one of the owners dies, their share of the property can be left to someone other than the other tenant.

Tied agents. A financial advisor who works for one company and only sells that company's financial products.

Title deeds. Paper documents showing the chain of ownership for land and property.

Title plan. A map produced by the Land Registry to record the general position of the boundaries of a registered property.

Title register. This list contains detailed property, house and land information, including ownership details, title number and leases. It is held and updated by the Land Registry.

Tracker mortgage. A type of mortgage that tracks the Bank of England's base rate. So, for example, if the base rate was 1%, your mortgage term may stipulate "base rate + 1.25%", making your monthly repayments 2.25%.

Under offer. If a property is said to be "under offer" the seller will have agreed an offer from a prospective buyer.

Underpinning. A solid foundation (usually made of reinforced concrete) laid below ground level to support or strengthen an existing building. It is mainly used to prevent further subsidence occurring.

Valuation report. A report undertaken to ascertain that the property is worth what the purchaser has agreed to pay.

Water Authority search. A search of the Water Authority's records to check whether the property is connected to mains drainage and to the mains water supply.

Will. A legal (usually written) declaration of a person's wishes regarding the disposal of his or her estate after death.

Woodworm. The wood-boring larva of the furniture beetle. If left untreated, these larvae can cause considerable structural damage.

Printed in Great Britain
by Amazon